D0880757

Montana and the West Series
Volume X

Camp on horseback at his farm.

Camp, Custer, and The Little Bighorn

A Collection of
Walter Mason Camp's Research Papers
on General George A. Custer's Last Fight

Compiled, edited, and annotated by
RICHARD G. HARDORFF

UPTON AND SONS, PUBLISHERS
El Segundo, California
1997

Also by Richard G. Hardorff:

The OglalaLakota Crazy Horse: A Preliminary Genealogical Study and Annotated Listing of Primary Sources (Mattituck, NY, 1985)

Markers, Artifacts and Indian Testimony: Preliminary Findings on the Custer Battle (Short Hills, NJ, 1985)

The Custer Battle Casualties: Burials, Exhumations and Reinterments (El Segundo, CA, 1989)

Lakota Recollections of the Custer Fight: New Sources of Indian-Military History (Spokane, WA, 1991)

Hokahey! A Good Day to Die! The Indian Casualties of the Custer Fight (Spokane, WA, 1993)

Cheyenne Memories of the Custer Fight: A Source Book (Spokane, WA, 1995)

Library of Congress Catalog Card Number
96-61462
ISBN Number 0-912783-25-7

After having listened to the story of the Little Bighorn Expedition from the lips of some of the men who participated therein, the current literature [in 1909] on the subject seemed to present such a tangle of fiction, fancy, fact and feeling that I formed an ambition to establish the truth. It occurred to me that the essential facts must rest in the minds of many men then living, and that these facts, if collected, would constitute fairly accurate history. This has been my plan—to gather my data from eyewitnesses.

—WALTER MASON CAMP

Contents

Illustrations

Maps

Introduction

June 25, 1876. While Americans in the East were preparing for the much anticipated centennial celebration of the Fourth of July, the West experienced the culmination of a culture clash which forever sealed the destiny of the adversaries. By nightfall of that bloody Sunday, five companies of Seventh Cavalry troopers lay dead among the dust-covered hills above the Little Bighorn, while a jubilant Indian force of Sioux and Cheyennes celebrated its pinnacle of military might. The historical imprint of this battle would last forever. Never, during all its armed confrontations with Native Americans, did so many American soldiers die in a single battle, having fought so desperately against such overwhelming odds, only to experience such complete defeat.

Although more than a century has passed, interest in the Battle of the Little Bighorn has not waned. To the contrary, more literature has been published on this single engagement than on any other confrontation in American warfare. Perhaps, the fascination with this battle stems from the spectrum of human emotions which encapsulates this tragic event. Fueled by controversy and speculation, this battle continues to appeal to the imagination to this very day.

Walter Mason Camp, too, was fascinated by this battle. Born at Camptown, Pennsylvania, on April 21, 1867, Walter M. Camp was the son of Treat Bosworth

Camp and Hannah A. Brown, both descendants of old colonial ancestry. Walter received his early education at Wyalusing, Pennsylvania, where, at the age of nine, he began employment as a fireman in a planing mill. At age sixteen, he was hired as a trackwalker by the Lehigh Valley Railroad, and commenced a railroad career which would span some forty-two years.

Camp entered Pennsylvania State College in 1887, and upon graduation as a civil engineer, he was hired as a surveyor by the Southern Pacific Company. After gaining experience as a draftsman, a construction engineer, a superintendent of operations and maintenance, and a section foreman, Camp entered graduate school at the University of Wisconsin in 1895. After graduation he taught for one year at the National School of Electricity in Chicago, and was then hired as inspector, and later superintendent, of track construction, for the Englewood and Chicago Electric Railway.

In 1897, Camp was hired as the editor of the *Railway and Engineering Review,* a monthly magazine containing technical railroad data, which had offices in the Manhattan Building on Dearborn Avenue in Chicago. Camp would stay on the editorial staff of this magazine the remainder of his life. The culmination of his professional career came in 1903, when he authored a two-volume study, *Notes on Track,* which was used as a text book by many institutions of higher education.

It is not known when, exactly, Camp first became interested in the study of the Custer Battle. However, a letter by him to Elizabeth B. Custer suggests that his study began in 1897. Camp's first visit to Custer Battlefield took place in 1903, during a vacation to the Little Bighorn country. Confronted by contradictions in publications on this historical event, Camp resolved to learn

This youthful image of Walter M. Camp was taken at his residence on
Union Avenue in Chicago, about 1910. *Courtesy John W. Husk Collection*

the facts by contacting survivors of the battle. He probably commenced this task in 1908, which is the earliest
date found on any of his research correspondence.

In September of 1908, Camp revisited the Little
Bighorn in presence of Daniel A. Knipe, a retired
sergeant of C Company who was dispatched in 1876 at
the very last moment, and who was thus spared his com-
rades' fate. Knipe related his experiences to Camp in
detail, and he also assisted him with the mapping of both
battlefields. Camp also met the Crow Indian, Curly, who
he interviewed as well.

During the winter, Camp had two lengthy interviews
with General Winfield S. Edgerly, and by the end of that
year he had discussed the Custer Battle with some eigh-

teen army officers and enlisted men, and also four Indians—Curly, Flying By, Turtle Rib, and Foolish Elk. He
was persuaded by the survivors to write a history of the
battle, which endeavor he intended to publish the following year.

The year 1909 proved to be quite busy for Camp due
to an increase in his work load. In between his field
assignments he was able to meet the old scout Fred Gerard, who was now bedridden by paralysis, his frail body
freed only by memories of a happier time long ago.

In May, Camp was sent on assignment in Montana
where he did engineering work for the anticipated exten-
sion of the Chicago, Milwaukee, and St. Paul Railway.
He stopped at Butte, Missoula, Miles City, and Deer
Lodge, to write up shop plants and to locate contractors
and railroad engineers. Camp did find time to make a
side trip to Boise, Idaho, to call on Colonel Charles A.
Varnum, which resulted in an interview which "lasted
from 3 p.m. in the afternoon to 2 a.m. the following
morning."

On his way back to Chicago, Camp stopped at Standing Rock Indian Reservation and talked with several
elderly Lakotas. One of these was Ring Cloud who, with
his brother, Appearing Bear, was enlisted in 1876 as a
US Indian Scout and who fought alongside Reno in the
valley. In July, Camp met with Major Thomas M.
McDougall, a timely interview which took place only
one week before the latter's death. Later in the year,
Camp was able to interview General Edward S. Godfrey.

Camp also located Peter Thompson in 1909. Formerly of C Company, Thompson's horse had broken
down near Reno Hill in 1876, and he, like Knipe, was
thus saved from the fate which befell Custer's five com-

panies. Camp made arrangements to meet Thompson at the battlefield in August. Present also was Daniel A. Knipe, who was accompanied by his wife Ann, the widow of First Sergeant Edwin Bobo who was slain in the fight.

Accompanying Camp was Stanislas Roy, a retired sergeant of A Company, whose travel expenses were paid for by Camp. Roy had told Camp of the kill site of Corporal John Foley, and Camp was anxious to have Roy show him the location on the battlefield. While at Crow Agency, Camp interviewed the Crow scout Goes Ahead, and he also had another interview with Curly while following Custer's route from the Crow's Nest to the battlefield.

During the months of January and February of 1910, Camp was on assignment in California to write editorials on the new Western Pacific Railway, and also the Santa Fe Railway in the southern part of that state. On his way to California, Camp stopped in Denver to interview Colonel Edward G. Mathey. While in Los Angeles he interviewed Major Charles A. DeRudio, and later paid his respects to Mrs. Myles Moylan in San Diego, her husband having died only a month earlier. On his return trip, Camp stopped in Austin, Texas, and interviewed Major Luther R. Hare.

In June of 1910, Camp managed to be present in Monroe, Michigan, for the dedication of the Custer monument. He was able to make his acquaintance with Elizabeth B. Custer who presented him a piece of red ribbon from the ribbon-cutting ceremony. The next month, July, Camp spent two weeks of his summer vacation on the Pine Ridge Reservation, in South Dakota, where he interviewed several elderly Oglalas, among whom Standing Bear and He Dog. Of the latter, Camp later wrote, "This old fellow is a judge of the Indian Court and had a splendid reputation among the white people for truthfulness. He has a splendid memory. I could not shake him on anything."

Leaving Pine Ridge, Camp journeyed to Crow Agency for yet another interview with Curly. The latter had promised Camp to accompany him on a trip through the Rosebud country. However, at the last moment Curly backed out, so Camp had to go alone. After crossing the divide, Camp drove his team of horses to the Rosebud Battlefield where General Crook had fought the same Indians who confronted Custer later in June of 1876. From there, Camp went to the Cheyenne Indian Reservation, on the Tongue River, where he interviewed several elderly Cheyennes, among whom Tall Bull, White Bull, and Two Moons. Camp recalled later that during this trip he had killed three rattlesnakes and two bull snakes, and that coyotes were howling at his tent every night.

After departing from the reservation, Camp drove his wagon down the Rosebud to the junction with the Yellowstone where he met George Herendeen, a scout who was with Custer's regiment in 1876. Herendeen took Camp back up the Rosebud, following the trail Custer had taken on his last campaign. After stopping at the Crow's Nest, the two men travelled across the divide and camped for the night at the ford where Reno crossed in his charge on the Indian village. The following morning, Herendeen showed Camp the spot where Charley Reynolds was killed, and then related his own experiences, both in the valley and on the hill.

Leaving Crow Agency, Camp returned to the East, visiting Fort Yates on the Standing Rock Indian Reservation where he talked to several old warriors. Reaching his office in Chicago in mid August, Camp was faced with a reduced work force, allowing him very little time for his contemplated history of the Seventh Cavalry. He therefore had to postpone any thought of publication.

In October 1910, Camp went to Denver to attend a railroad convention, and while there, he called again on Colonel Edward G. Mathey who granted him a second interview. Camp also made a side trip to the Washita Battlefield with Ben Clark, Custer's scout in 1868, and mapped the battlefield. At the end of the year, Camp mailed a circular letter to Grand Army posts and other military facilities in the hope of finding some more veterans of the Seventh Cavalry.

The year 1911 started out with an editorial assignment on new railroad construction in St. Paul. Camp then took a business trip to Portland, Oregon, and was gone a month, and was back in Chicago in March. In order to get material for the annual publication, *Maintenance of Way,* Camp went to Spokane, Washington, and while there he interviewed some of the elderly Nez Perce Indians.

During the same year, Camp also visited the battle sites of Bear Paw Mountains, Wounded Knee, Washita, and the Arickaree Fork of the Republican—all of which installed in him an urgency to record eyewitness information before the participants of these fights passed away. He therefore decided to expand his Seventh Cavalry history to include "all of the Indian fighting on the plains, from start to finish." Camp entrusted to Daniel A. Knipe that he intended to make this history as thorough as he could, but that he also had to make a living as he went along.

During his summer vacation in 1911, Camp spent five weeks on the Sioux reservations, compiling recollections of historical events. Wrote Camp, "I get a great deal of light about the fighting, from the Indians, many of whom take a lively interest in my work. They impress me as truthful men, with good memories, and, whatever one can say about the Indians, they are no fools."

In February 1912, Camp was back on the Cheyenne reservation in Montana where Willis Rowland assisted him once again with the translations of interviews with elderly Cheyennes. During his summer vacation, in July, Camp spent several weeks at Standing Rock, North Dakota, where he obtained additional information from the Sioux, among whom White Bull, One Bull, and Flying By. He also visited the Fort Berthold Reservation to interview a number of the old Ree Indian scouts.

In between his field research and editorial assignments, Camp was able to find time to purchase a two-acre farm in Lake Village, Indiana. Camp used this investment as rental property, hoping to eventually settle on this farm after his retirement.

In January of 1913, Camp was on editorial assignment in the Northwest.

While there, he compiled a number of interviews on the Nez Perce Campaign of 1877. During his vacation in September, Camp returned to the Rosebud country, in Montana, where he mapped the battle sites of the Yellowstone Expedition of 1874. After making his usual stop at the Cheyenne reservation, Camp crossed the divide and travelled to Crow Agency where he interviewed Curly once more. By the end of this year, Camp had gathered substantial data on all the Indian campaigns of the Seventh Cavalry. Reflecting on his progress, Camp wrote, "The only drawback with me is lack of time. I am keeping up my investigations, whenever I find a new source of information, and hope, before many years, if God let me live, to do justice to the subject."

Little is known of Camp's activities in 1914 and 1915. Perhaps his editorial assignments had increased to such an extent that very little time was available to him to pursue his avocational interests. We do know that the volume of Camp's correspondence greatly reduced during these years. However, Camp did manage to accompany General Anson Mills and General Charles Morton on a trip to locate the battle site of Slim Buttes. After travelling some 500 miles, they were unsuccessful in locating the site. In the same month, September, Camp was able to spent time in Montana where he visited with his favorite tribe, the Cheyennes.

Early in 1916, Camp attended the banquet of the Order of the Indian Wars as guest of General Anson Mills. He also attended the twenty-fifth anniversary of the graduation of his class at the Pennsylvania State College, near Bellefonte, Pennsylvania, at the geographical center of that state. Later he visited his widowed mother, who was in poor health. During the same year, he would visit her four more times, each time travelling from Chicago to Pennsylvania, the last trip being made to attend her funeral.

In March 1916, Camp was invited by General Edward S. Godfrey to accompany him over Custer's trail to the battlefield, to attend the celebration of the fortieth anniversary. Camp had gone over this trail twice already, once with George Herendeen in 1910. In four different years since then, Camp had visited the Cheyenne Indian Reservation, which he intended to do again. Camp also made preparations for the placement of a marker at the site were Charley Reynolds was killed. The expenses of this monument were to be shared by Camp and George Bird Grinnell. At Camp's suggestion, plans were also being formulated to place bronze markers at the burial sites of Little Wolf and Dull Knife, on the Cheyenne reservation, Camp having great admiration for the memory of these two men.

On June 15, 1916, Camp left Pennsylvania for Montana for the much-anticipated trip to Custer Battlefield. He probably met General Godfrey at the town of Rosebud, situated along the Yellowstone, which was a station on the Northern Pacific line. In Godfrey's party were several guests, among which were George Bird Grinnell, who Camp had met before, and Laton A. Huffman, a frontier photographer. The transportation consisted of two ambulances drawn by four horses each, placed at Godfrey's service at the remount station at Ft. Keogh, which also assigned four soldiers to serve Godfrey at his every command.

Camp had considerable outdoors' experience, and he had advised Godfrey to bring a woolen blanket and a poncho, a pair of lace boots, or leggings with substantial shoes, and for utensils a tin plate, a cup, a knife, a fork and a spoon. Camp was in the habit of wearing a broad-brimmed hat on the plains for protection against the sun. He rode a saddle horse, and he always took a camera along, having acquired a great deal of expertise in the use of the latter as magazine editor.

The trip up the Rosebud would prove to be a disappointment to Godfrey. The journey was made in the midst of a storm which lasted four days. The country was flooded and three bridges were washed out. At some places the stream was half of a mile wide, making the roads impassible and requiring long detours, one taking as much as sixteen miles. On the very first day Godfrey was drenched by the torrential rains. He caught a cold which made him feel miserable throughout the entire trip.

In this Huffman photograph, Walter M. Camp (second from right)
poses near Gen. Godfrey's coach in the Rosebud Valley, June 1916.
The young boy was probably the son of John B. McRea.
Courtesy Montana Historical Society

The first stop was made some twelve miles up the
Rosebud, at a log house owned by Charles Bray, a
rancher who Camp knew very well. Since the entire area
was flooded, Godfrey failed to locate the site where
Custer camped on the night of June 22, 1876. The next
morning the party of dignitaries travelled up the Rosebud and camped for the night at the homes of Scotch
sheep herders, near a location which Godfrey thought
was Custer's bivouac on the night of June 23. The next
stopping place was at the little town of Busby where the
party probably stayed at the home of Reverent L. A. Lin-
scheid, a Mennonite preacher. However, the Busby
location did not remind Godfrey of the site of Custer's
last bivouac on the Rosebud.

The following morning, June 24, 1916, the party travelled to the mouth of Davis Creek, a dry fork pointed out to Camp by George Herendeen and the Crows in previous years as the streambed used by Custer to ascent to the divide. Godfrey, however, disputed the validity of the claim. Stubborn by nature, Godfrey ignored Camp's knowledge of Custer's route, and decided to search for Custer's trail farther up the Rosebud. Accompanied by Laton A. Huffman only, Godfrey followed the latter stream for some distance and then ascended Thompson Creek, riding some fifteen miles before they finally reached the divide. They got lost in the mountains and tired out, but eventually reached a lonely ranch house where they rested for several hours. Some sympathetic ranchers provided Godfrey and Huffman with a buggy and drove them to the Little Bighorn, reaching the stream some five miles above the ford where Reno crossed the river in 1876.

During Godfrey's absence, Camp and Grinnell, along with the military escort, ascended Davis Creek and camped on the divide, having a leisure time, the soldiers doing all the camp chores. When dusk fell, Camp went out on horseback to see if he, perhaps, could find Godfrey. In this, Camp was unsuccessful, and it was not until the following day that he met Godfrey who had arrived at Custer Battlefield in an exhausted condition, just in time for the commencement of the celebration.

Godfrey later told Camp that he, Godfrey, and Huffman had travelled all night, and that they were worn out, having had nothing to eat and having ridden some thirty miles out of their way. Godfrey admitted that the Thompson route was not the route Custer had taken; that he, Godfrey, had gone the wrong way and that the entire trip had turned out to be a disappointment to

This photograph was taken by Laton A. Huffman on the McRea ranch
in the valley of the Rosebud, Montana, in June 1916. Standing
from left to right: Walter M. Camp, Dr. George B. Grinnell,
John B. McRea (?), and Gen. Edward S. Godfrey.
Courtesy Montana Historical Society.

him; that his failure was his own fault, and that he did
not bear any ill feelings to anyone.

The main event on June 25 was Godfrey's speech,
given to an assemblage of 5000 people, beside some 800
Indians, nearly all of whom were Crows, although there
were some 100 Cheyennes of whom many were survivors of the battle. Other speakers were Goes Ahead,
who was one of Custer's scouts and who was interpreted
by Russell White Bear, and Two Moons, a Cheyenne
chief, who was interpreted by Willis Rowland. This was
Two Moons' last public appearance because he passed
away in April of the following year.

On the next day, Godfrey took Camp over the battlefields to explain his part in the engagements. The following morning, Godfrey left for Missoula, Montana, to

give a speech at the unveiling of a monument. Camp, however, returned to the Tongue River Reservation where he met some of his Cheyenne friends. Later in the year, in October, Camp passed through Colony, Oklahoma, where he visited George Bent for three days. However, Camp did not interview any of the old Cheyennes as they were away on visits. He did meet Edmond Guerrier who gave him an account of the Kidder Affair.

During the year 1916, Camp had been extremely busy. In the later part of the year he returned to Pennsylvania to settle the estate of his deceased mother. In addition, Camp twice went to New York and made other trips to Oklahoma to finish editorial assignments for the *Railway Review*. As a result, his personal correspondence, which had been laying on his desk since March 1916, was not answered by him until February of the following year. Asked about the progress of his historical investigations, Camp wrote, "I fear it will be two years or more before I get to the publication of it. I could not publish it now, even if I had it completely written, owing to the forbidding prices of printing, binding, and the double price of paper, binding cloth, etc. This European war is just knocking the publishing business all to pieces."

In 1917, Camp was invited by Peter Thompson to accompany him on a hunting expedition in the Big Horn Mountains. Thompson was a Medal of Honor winner, and he was one of the last men to see Custer alive. On his way to Montana, Camp stopped off in North Dakota to interview several Oglalas and Ree scouts, arriving in Sheridan, Wyoming, on August 4, 1917, to spent ten days with Thompson. However, the ten days turned into eighteen days as a result of the slow-moving outfit, which was in the habit of breaking bivouac late each day.

Looking west, this sweeping view from Reno Hill was taken by Laton A.
Huffman in June 1916, and shows Walter M. Camp (left) and Gen.
Edward S. Godfrey (right) descending toward the Retreat
Ravine, identified by the stone marker for Dr. DeWolf.
Courtesy Montana Historical Society

Consequently, Camp missed a planned meeting with
George Bird Grinnell on the Cheyenne reservation and,
being pressed for time, Camp did not get a chance to
interview any of the Cheyennes.

On August 24, Camp placed a marker on the divide
between the Rosebud and the Little Bighorn, at the
point where Custer and the Seventh Cavalry crossed the
divide on June 25, 1876. This marker was placed at the
request of the Montana State Historical Society, which
was represented by Mr. M.L. Wilson who was present
when the marker was set. This marker consisted of a circular brass tablet, eight inches in diameter, riveted to a
square plate of cast-iron, one inch thick, the latter set
three feet in the ground and projecting a foot above

ground. The tablet laid horizontally on top of the pillar and had the following stamped inscription, "General George A. Custer and the Seventh U.S. Cavalry Crossed the Divide at This Point, June 25, 1876."

In a statement filed with the Montana State Historical Society on October 17, 1917, Camp explained that the point where Custer crossed the divide and where the marker was placed, was first shown to him by the Crow Indian, Curly, on August 4, 1909, and also by George Herendeen, on July 27, 1910, both individuals having identified the same place at different times. In addition, Herendeen revisited the divide shortly after the placement of the marker and confirmed to Camp its correct location.

After placing the tablet on the divide, Camp hurried to Busby on August 24, arriving there late at night, hoping that perhaps Grinnell would still be in town. However, as a result of Camp's delay in the mountains, Grinnell had left the Cheyenne reservation for the season and had departed for Glacier Park. The following morning, Camp departed for the Yellowstone to take the Northern Pacific back East, thoroughly upset with himself for having wasted so much time on a pleasure trip, at the sacrifice of his historical work.

Reflecting on the progress of his research near the end of 1917, Camp wrote Elizabeth Custer, "I have visited the [Custer] battlefield in nine different years, sometimes staying more than a week at a time. As to the trail between the Yellowstone and the Little Bighorn, I have been over all of it five times, for the purpose of historical study, and I have been over the west end of it (between the divide and the Little Bighorn) eight times. I have interviewed more than sixty survivors of Maj. Reno's command, including eight officers, and more than 150

Walter M. Camp (left) and Gen. Edward S. Godfrey near Sharp Shoot-
ers Ridge, just north of the Retreat Ravine, which can be seen
on the left. Photo by Laton A. Huffman, June 1916.
Courtesy Montana Historical Society.

Indian survivors of this battle. I do not write the above
boastfully, but am anxious that you should know that my
work has been painstaking. In all these investigations I
have cared for nothing but facts."

In 1918, the office staff at the *Railway Review* was
reduced by the departure of one of the editors. Although
a replacement was eventually hired, Camp was assigned
the additional responsibilities, leaving very little time for
research. However, during his summer vacation Camp
was able once again to free himself from city life and his
demanding editorial job, to spend time at Fort Laramie
and the site of the Grattan Fight, interviewing old-
timers. He also visted Pine Ridge and Cheyenne River
where he was known by the name *Wicati,* the Sioux word

for "camp." We also know that he revisited Custer Battlefield. This was the last time he stood on Monument Hill, his eyes sweeping the hallowed ground below, to reflect, with feelings of intimacy, on the battle which had been the subject of his study for so many years of his life.

As a result of the race riots in Chicago, in 1919, one of the *Railway Review* editors was called into service with the National Guard, just as Camp was ready to leave for his summer vacation. Much to his disappointment, the additional work load transferred to Camp would not allow him to go West, the first time ever that he missed an "Indian Campaign" since 1903. Reflecting on these vacations, Camp wrote, "I have usually been able each summer to get enough of the plains atmosphere into my system to keep busy looking up references and writing letters to survivors the remainder of the 'campaign' year." Despite this heavy work load, Camp did find time to attend the annual meeting of the Order of the Indian Wars, having been nominated by General W.C. Brown to become the first Honorary Companion.

On January 17, 1920, Camp again attended the annual meeting of the Order of the Indian Wars, this time as a guest of General Anson Mills. After the banquet, Camp was the guest speaker and delivered an address on the topic of the battlefields of the Indian wars. Camp had visited some thirty-five of these battlefields and found that only three of these had been marked.

On July 30, 1920, Camp was finally able to take his annual vacation on the plains. Freeing himself from the restraints of city life and his editorial work, Camp travelled alone, adhering to an itinerary which was planned to last six weeks. This trip, taken by automobile, took him to South Dakota where he visited some of his old Sioux friends. Camp then went on to Slim Buttes, to be present with General Mills at the dedication of a monument on the battlefield.

From Slim Buttes, Camp drove to Crook's battlefield on the Rosebud where he placed nine government markers for the soldiers slain at this location on June 17, 1876. Their graves had never been marked and the skeletal remains had been plowed out by ranchers. From there Camp drove back down the Rosebud, stopping at the Tongue River Reservation, to talk to the elderly Cheyennes. Upon his return East, Camp applied for a government stone for Frank Grouard, a scout for General Crook, who was buried in St. Louis.

In February 1921, Camp was again invited by General Anson Mills to attend the banquet of the Order of the Indian Wars, which invitation he accepted. However, he declined the invitation by General Godfrey to attend the forty-fifth anniversary of the Custer Battle, in Montana. He cited for his reason an increased work load at the *Railway Review* due to the feeble condition of his employer.

Conditions in his personal life, too, started to take a toll on Camp. The health of his wife had declined, and she refused to move onto the farm at Lake Village in Indiana, which property had been bought by the couple for retirement. In addition, the economic conditions relating to farm investments took a turn for the worse due to the scarcity of farm laborers, who were offered much higher wages for manual labor in the cities.

Although Camp had hired a family to run his farm in 1912, by 1923 most farm laborers had moved to the cities, making it necessary for Camp to attend to the farm business himself. As a consequence, Camp took a leave of absence from his editorial job, eventually writing only weekly editorials which he submitted to the *Review* by mail from Lake Village.

Walter M. Camp and his trusted companion on his farm at Lake
Village, Indiana, where Camp resided alone during the last few
years of his life. *Courtesy John W. Husk Collection.*

Reflecting on the economic depression, Camp wrote,
"More than half the time I have not even had a single
helper, and have had to do milking and other chores, as
well as to attend to the growing crops. I have been on the
jump, from daylight to dark, all summer. Other farmers
this distance [55 miles] from Chicago were in the same
fix, and a good many farms here about have been
allowed to stand idle for want of labor to work them."

While his ailing wife resided at the Chicago residence,
Camp was "stuck" on the farm, attending to a business
for which he now cared very little. Eventually, a decision
was reached by the couple to sell the farm, including the
Holstein cattle and other livestock. The buildings, however, were somewhat dilapidated, a condition which was

duly noted by a prospective buyer, in 1924. As a result, the sale did not materialize, forcing Camp to spent the remainder of the year repairing farm buildings and filling silos.

Camp remained optimistic about the prospect of selling his farm property, which had kept him from returning to his beloved West for the last four years. Wrote Camp, "As soon as I can get loose I intend to spent several months in the West and try to renew my acquaintances out there. I have a Reo 'Speed Wagon' which is just the thing for camping. It can carry a load, runs as fast as a touring car, and rides easy. I wish I might, with good prospects, look forward to a long trip out there next year."

By the end of 1924, Camp was still living at Lake Village. Wrote he, "[I] hope to sell before another year. If I can do that I will be in good shape to go to work again on my western studies. I have in mind to take an auto-truck and go west for a trip of six months, or longer, just as soon as I can get free from this farm work, which I care nothing about." Camp's dream never materialized. He suddenly took ill and was hospitalized in Kankakee, Illinois, where he died unexpectedly on August 3, 1925.

In 1933, Walter Camp's widow sold her husband's research papers to General William C. Brown. General Brown eventually transferred the papers to Robert S. Ellison, an avid collector of Western Americana and who at one time was chairman of the Historical Landmark Commission of Wyoming.

Upon Ellison's death in 1945, a large part of his papers and library was donated to the Lilly Library of Indiana University, in Indiana, which was his alma mater. Included in this donation were some of Walter Camp's research notes. In 1967, Ellison's widow bequeathed additional materials to Lilly Library, among which a more substantial segment of Camp's notes.

A small segment of the Camp notes, and a few papers from Ellison's collection, was also donated to the Denver Public Library. The remaining Camp papers, consisting of letters, interviews, and the bulk of the notes, were purchased in 1968 by the Harold B. Lee Library of Brigham Young University, in Utah.

In 1976, Brigham Young University Press published fifty-four of Camp's interviews on the Custer Battle, under the editorship of Dr. Kenneth Hammer, of the University of Wisconsin at Whitewater. Dr. Hammer's thorough knowledge of the subject matter resulted in the acclaimed publication, *Custer in '76: Walter M. Camp's Notes on the Custer Fight,* which has become a classic in its field.

In 1986, the National Park Service at Custer Battlefield National Monument received a donation of Camp letters from Mrs. Naomi Dettmar and her brother, Keith Roberts, Sr. This donation contained five lengthy interviews with Sioux Indians which were included by me in *Lakota Recollections of the Custer Fight,* published in 1991. A companion work, *Cheyenne Memories of the Custer Fight,* published in 1995, contains several of Camp's interviews with the Cheyennes.

In 1993, Denver Public Library received a donation of Camp interviews from Paul Harbaugh. These interviews cover a wide range of topics, and a portion of them were edited by the donor and Bruce Liddic and published under the title *Camp on Custer,* in 1995.

In view of all these acquisitions, one wonders if more Camp materials will surface. We know that some of the letters from Camp's correspondents are missing, chief among which are those written by Elizabeth B. Custer.

Of unkown date and origin, this studio portrait is one of only two portraits known to exist of Walter M. Camp. *Courtesy John W. Husk Collection.*

There are also a number of interviews missing on Custer's last fight, which is also the case with Camp's field diaries, which have not been located as yet.

Although the more revealing Camp interviews on the Little Bighorn Fight have been published, there still remains a number of short interviews which, if printed, would be of interest to students of the battle. The present publication contains thirty-six of these short interviews, which have been extensively annotated with Camp's unpublished notes and letters.

This work was made possible through the kind assistance of numerous people, who have earned my enduring gratitude. The following individuals were especially helpful. Saundra Taylor, Curator of Manuscripts, Lilly Library, Indiana University, Bloomington, Indiana, for her permission to publish items from the Camp Manuscripts; Scott H. Duvall, Chair, Special Collections and Manuscripts Department, Harold B. Lee Library, Brigham Young University, Provo, Utah, for his permission to publish items from the Camp Collection; and also Leda Farley, departmental secretary, Harold B. Lee Library, who graciously assisted me on so many occasions; Eleanor M. Gehres, Manager, Western History Department, Denver Public Library, for her permission to publish from the Camp Papers in the Robert Ellison Collection; Father Paul Manhart, S.J., Holy Rosary Mission, Pine Ridge, South Dakota, for his assistance with the Lakota language; Doug McChristian, Chief Historian, Little Bighorn Battlefield National Monument, Montana, for his permission to publish items from the Camp Collection; and Kitty Deernose, Museum Technician, also of the Little Bighorn National Monument, who as always skillfully assisted me with my photo research, as did Sandy Barnard of Terre Haute, Indiana, and John W. Husk of Englewood, Colorado, and, especially, Dr. James Brust of San Pedro, California; and lastly, my wife Renee, who I like to thank for her cheerful assistance throughout this enjoyable project.

Richard G. Hardorff
Genoa, Illinois
January 1, 1997

INTERVIEWS

Interview with Frank Geist
[No date][1]

Two companies of 17th Infantry left at Powder River with wagon train. I Co. 6th Infantry along and went on steamer. Camp was on south side of the Yellowstone, just below the mouth of Powder, on big flat, among many of the new rattlesnakes. Recruits had no horses [upon] leaving Ft. Lincoln and walked out, catching rides on wagons some of the time. Many of the men left at Powder were left there by reason of being without mounts. Third day out a wagon tipped over containing Capt. Benteen's private property and spilled some of his cherry brandy. Custer had his pack of greyhounds along.[2]

When [we] got into the bad lands, the band boys got tired of playing and pretended to have got sand in their instruments; so, on occasion Custer put them at pick and shovel with the pioneer corps. Band was mounted and remained at Powder River with their horses. Sure Botzer[3] was Acting First Sergeant[4] from time left Ft. Lincoln. Says DeRudio the only one in regiment who carried saber. Custer had no sword. Carried a rifle.

---

[1]Camp MSS, field notes, box 2, folder 10, Little Bighorn, Battle of 1876, II, Lilly Library, Indiana University, Bloomington, IN, hereafter cited as IU Library, IN. Born in 1854 in Wurtzburg, Germany, Frank J. Geist enlisted in St. Louis on April 14, 1876, and served in G Company until January 30, 1879, when disability forced his discharge as a Private of good character. Geist was on detached service from June 15, 1876, at the Yellowstone Depot.

[2](Camp note:) Godfrey says one of Custer's dogs jumped onto Godfrey's porch on June 25, 1885. This dog came back from the 1876 expedition to Ft. Lincoln nearly starved and was kept around guard house at Ft. Lincoln. After [wards] the cavalry moved to Yates and dog taken along and kept with guard ho [use]. Dog recognized Godfrey and acted friendly with him and Godfrey's children. (Manuscript 57, Walter Mason Camp, transcript, p. 184, Harold B. Lee Library, Brigham Young University, UT, hereafter cited as BYU.

[3]Sergeant Edward Botzer served in G Company and went into combat with Reno's battalion on the valley floor. He was slain on the east bank of the river, near the retreat crossing, his body being found not far from Lt. Hodgson's remains. See A.L. DeVoto to W.M. Camp, 11/15/1917, Walter M. Camp Collection, Little Bighorn Battlefield National Monument, National Park Service, hereafter cited as LBHNM.

[4]First Sergeant Edward Garlick had been absent on furlough since April 14, 1876.

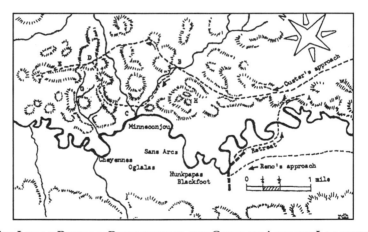

THE LITTLE BIGHORN BATTLEFIELDS, AND COMPANY ACTIVITY LOCATIONS

A) Reno Hill

B) Luce Ridge, from where E and F were sent to the river

C) Minneconjou Ford

D) Calhourn Hill, where members from C and L perished

E) Where I and surviving members of C and L perished

F) Custer Hill, site of the "Last Stand"

G) Deep Ravine, where 28 men were slain on the bottom

H) Weir Point, farthest advance of the Reno-Benteen force

INTERVIEW WITH HARVEY A. FOX
AND JOHN A. BAILEY

[No date][1]

Harvey A. Fox says Bob Jackson[2] was sent back to Ft. A. Lincoln with a dispatch from the Little Missouri and did not get any farther than Powder River by June 25. Says that when Custer got to the Little Missouri he gave strict orders that there should be no unnecessary shooting about the camp. In disregard of this, Bob Jackson went down to the river and blazed away at some ducks. Custer was unable at once to contrive what form of punishment would be suitable, but finally decided to get rid of him for the time being by sending him back with a dispatch.

Harvey A. Fox, D Co., was left at the Powder River. Says Bob Jackson was sent back with dispatch from the Little Missouri and never got to the Little Bighorn. Says Cross[3] was first to reach the Powder with one or two Rees. [Cross] could give no satisfactory account of the fighting, but seemed to think all were killed. Billy Cross was a halfbreed Sioux. Bob Jackson was at Colorado Springs in 1899. His white wife wanted him to get away from there as he was drinking...

John A. Bailey says Bob Jackson was not at the Little Bighorn, June 25 or 26. Says that at the Little Missouri River, Reno had him, Jackson, standing on a barrel as punishment for some offense or other, and they understood that at about this time he was sent back with a dispatch.

---

[1]Camp MSS, field notes, unclassified envelope 44, IU Library, IN. Born in North Carolina in 1848, Harvey A. Fox enlisted on July 27, 1871, and was assigned to D Company. He was on detached service from June 15, 1876, at the Yellowstone Depot, and was dis-

charged on July 27, 1876, at the mouth of the Rosebud upon expiration of his enlistment, as a Private. In 1909, Fox resided on the Blackfoot Reservation, having married the mother of Bob and Billy Jackson, a Piegan woman who was then 75 years old.

Born in Illinois in 1845, John A. Bailey enlisted in 1870 and was assigned to B Company. After serving two enlistments, he was discharged on December 9, 1880, at Ft. Yates, Dakota, as a Saddler of very good character. On March 17, 1878, Capt. Thomas M. McDougall recommended Bailey for the Medal of Honor for gallant behavior during the battle, especially on June 26, when Bailey, unselfishly, offered his rifle pit to McDougall to insure the latter's safety, thereby exposing himself to heavy Indian fire after a charge by the troops. The Board of Officers, however, did not endorse the recommendation and the medal was not awarded.

[2]Born in 1854, Bob Jackson was the son of a white trader and a mixed-blood Piegan Indian woman, and was the older brother of William Jackson. Bob Jackson attended the Santee Indian Mission School in Nebraska and on June 24, 1874, enlisted as an Indian scout, recruited for the Black Hills expedition. He remained continuously in service until June 24, 1876, when he was discharged at Ft. Lincoln upon expiration of his enlistment. He later served intermittently for several years as a courier and a scout at the Glendive Supply Depot and at Ft. Keogh. One of his wives was Mary Miles, who lived at Castle, Montana, in the 1910s. This marriage resulted in the births of Millie, Andrew, John, and Jean Jackson. Elija Uhlic Browning was another daughter of Bob Jackson; she, however, was born from a different marriage.

[3]William "Billy" Cross was a mixed-blood Sioux interpreter who was born in Dakota Territory about 1854. It was said of him by his contemporaries that he had a reputation of honesty and trustworthiness, and that he was well versed in the English language. He enlisted at Ft. Lincoln as a scout on April 17, 1875, for the first of three consecutive six-month terms. He was present with Reno in the valley fight and served with the Army during the remainder of the 1876 expedition. He was subsequently hired as a scout at Tongue River Cantonment where he intermittently served until 1880. His experiences in the valley fight were recorded by a newspaper correspondent on July 4, 1876, and published in the *Chicago Tribune* of July 15, 1876.

Interview with Patrick Corcoran
[No date][1]

About Dennis Lynch[2] giving up [his] horse. Is he sure it was Lynch and how long had he known him? Very sure. Knew him well. Did Lynch go from boat to battlefield when Terry[3] came up? Don't know. At Rosebud on June 22 was Corcoran on headquarters detail? Yes. Did any scout go with Terry or Nowlan[4] on the boat? Don't know. Custer told Lynch he would give him a few minutes to think it over, and said: "Get on the boat and look after my baggage. Roll down my bed and tumble into it. You will not have anything to do."

---

[1]Camp MSS, field notes, unclassified envelope 130, IU Library, IN. Born in Canada in 1844, Patrick Corcoran enlisted in K Company in 1867, and reenlisted for a second five-year term in August of 1872. He was wounded in the right shoulder during the hilltop fight, early in the morning of June 26, and was transferred to Ft. Lincoln on the steamer *Far West*. Corcoran was discharged for disability in 1877. A second, short interview with Corcoran may be found in Hammer, *Custer in '76: Walter Camp's Notes on the Custer Fight* (Provo: Brigham Young University Press, 1976), p. 150. The Camp Collection at BYU contains several letters written by Corcoran to Camp.

[2]Born in Cumberland, Maryland in 1848, Dennis Lynch served in the Civil War and afterwards enlisted in F Company, in 1866. After serving two terms, he was discharged on August 3, 1876, at the mouth of the Rosebud, upon expiration of services, as a Private of excellent character. In a letter to Camp, dated 11/28/190[8], housed at BYU, Lynch wrote that he was with the pack train on June 25, a statement which he reiterated during his interview with Camp in 1909, and published in Hammer, *Custer in '76*, pp. 138-40. However, there exists some doubt about the veracity of Lynch's statements. Camp learned from George Herendeen that on June 22, 1876, "Custer gave him his choice of horses ridden by about 20 men of headquarters detail. The choice fell on the horse of Dennis Lynch. Lynch hesitated to give him up, but finally consented, and

Custer told him to get on the boat and look after his luggage, which Lynch did and afterward said that this act of Custer's saved his life." (Ibid, p. 221.) Herendeen's statement was confirmed by Corcoran, and indirectly also by James M. Rooney, a fellow member of Lynch's F Company, who wrote Camp on 2/23/1910 (BYU): "As to Lynch, I think the Troop records will show where he was, not wishing to cause any hard feelings to [an] old comrade. I will try to [say, however,] that he has been loading you to a certain extent."

[3]Gen. Alfred H. Terry, who commanded the Department of Dakota.

[4]Lt. Henry J. Nowlan, who served as Regimental Quartermaster from March 1, 1872, to June 25, 1876.

INTERVIEW WITH EDWARD G. MATHEY
January 19, 1910[1]

Hare[2] met him on a little knoll where Mathey [had] stopped waiting for packs and McDougall,[3] to get where he thought would be a good place to make a stand if attacked. (This knoll, he thinks, was on the north side of the north branch of Sundance Creek[4] because he recalls the packs coming off some of the mules in crossing the dry ravine.) He asked Hare how Custer was getting along and Hare said "They are giving us hell." Said [that] Hodgson[5] and McIntosh[6] [were] killed, Reno [was] whipped, and many men killed in the valley, and wanted to hurry up ammunition.

When Mathey got up the bluffs, Reno was much exited and ordered French to take a detail and go down and bring up Hodgson's body. When French [was] halfway down, Reno ordered him back and said [they] must go and find Custer.[7] He then held up a bottle of whiskey and showed it to Mathey and said: "Look here, I got half a bottle yet." Mathey was then under the impression that Reno was under the influence, but does not wish to be quoted. Says also that Reno was much exited.[8]

After Terry came up, went into camp in bottom and Mathey was there with pack train while burying the dead. Reno formed remnant of C, E, I, F, and L into a company and put [this unit] under Mathey, Mathey having been relieved of the pack train by Nowlan, who had come up with Terry as one of his staff. The first day, DeRudio[9] who did not like to serve under Moylan,[10] was appointed as assistant to Mathey. Mathey had Old Comanche[11] before Keogh did.

On the night of June 24 they camped, and about 11 p.m. Custer started again and proceeded along in darkness. Finally Lieut. Mathey rode up to him and said that he was much concerned about the pack train. The mules were tired and were strung out on the trail a long way back in the darkness, and he was afraid that unless a halt was made to give him a chance to get them up, many of them might be lost. Custer said all right, [to] do the best he could, and he would not go much farther. Accordingly, Custer halted the command just before daylight.

Henry J. Nowlan went on the boat with Gen. Terry and did not get to battlefield until June 27. Mathey says that on Reno Hill on June 25 the Indians were already firing before he got the pack train corralled.

---

[1]Born in France in 1837, Edward G. Mathey served during the Civil War in the Indiana Volunteer Infantry and was mustered out in 1865 with the rank of Major. He received a commission as Second Lieutenant in the Seventh Cavalry on September 24, 1867, and was promoted to First Lieutenant on May 10, 1870, and to Captain on September 30, 1877. He retired with the rank of Major on Decem-

ber 11, 1896, for disabilities incurred in the line of duty, and was promoted to Lieut. Colonel, USA, retired, on April 23, 1904. Mathey died in Denver on July 17, 1915, and was interred in the Arlington National Cemetery, in Virginia. Regularly assigned to M Company, Mathey had charge of the pack train from June 22 till June 27, 1876. See also Hammer, *Custer in '76*, pp. 78-79, which contains a later interview with Mathey. The Camp Collection at BYU contains three of his letters.

[2]Regularly assigned to K Company, Lt. Luther R. Hare was attached to the Detachment of US Indian Scouts on June 24, 1876, to assist Lt. Charles A. Varnum, Chief of Scouts. On the afternoon of June 25, Mathey was appointed Acting Adjutant by Reno to fill the vacancy created by the death of Lt. Benjamin H. Hodgson.

[3]Captain Thomas M. McDougall, who commanded B Company, which served as an escort to Mathey's pack train.

[4]Known by a variety of names in early nomenclature, Sundance Creek is presently identified as Reno Creek.

[5]Normally assigned to McDougall's B Company, Lt. Benjamin H. Hodgson was serving as Acting Adjutant of Reno's battalion when he was killed on the east bank, near the retreat crossing.

[6]Lt. Donald McIntosh, commanding G Company, was slain during the retreat from the valley floor.

[7]Captain Thomas H. French, commanding M Company. However, Mathey is mistaken in his recollection: it was not French, but Varnum who was told by Reno to bury Hodgson's remains. This order was given on Reno's return from the riverbank where he recovered some personal belongings from Hodgson's body. However, as a result of the troop movement to Weir Point, this order was rescinded before Varnum could complete his task. Notwithstanding, Hodgson's remains were eventually buried; but the question remains as to who carried the body up the hill, and who buried it. Capt. McDougall testified at the Reno Court of Inquiry, in 1878, that he, and Private Stephen L. Ryan and Farrier James E. Moore, both of B Company, carried Hodgson's body from the river into the breastworks on the night of June 26, leaving the remains in one of the vacated trenches on the southside of Reno Hill, for burial on the 27th. McDougall told Walter Camp the same story in 1909, except that he identified the names of the men with him as Sergeant Benjamin C. Criswell, Private Stephen L. Ryan, and Saddler John A. Bailey.

Strangely enough, several officers of the Montana Column saw

Hodgson's body still laying on the riverbank on the morning of June 27. Their observations are corroborated by Private Thomas W. Coleman, B Company, who entrusted to his diary: "This morning, after sunrise on June 27, I went over the battlefield on the east side of the river and the first person I saw was Lieutenant Hodgson of my company. He was shot twice with ball and once with arrow. Several other bodies lay close by. I buried the Lieutenant on a nice knoll overlooking the river, with a cedar tree at his head." The accuracy of this statement is born out by an account of the battle written by Augustus L. DeVoto, formerly of B Company: "The next day, the 27th, some of us were detailed to go over Reno's battleground, and find the missing or dead. I, with Sergeant Criswell and three other men, went to look for Lieutenant Hodgerson [sic]. We found his body on the bank, about twenty feet from the water. His body was naked. He had been shot in the temple and groin. Nearby were several dead members of G Troop. One, I remember, was Sergeant Botzer, First Sergeant of G Troop. We laid Lieutenant Hodgerson's body across our carbines and carried it to camp. We dug a grave, wrapped his body in a blanket, and buried it on the hill. We planted a sapling there to mark his grave."

What conclusion may we draw from these statements? It appears that McDougall erred in his recollection, and that Hodgson's body was not recovered until the morning of June 27, after the arrival of Terry's troops. The men who recovered the body consisted of a squad of B Company: Privates Thomas W. Coleman, Augustus L. DeVoto, and Stephen L. Ryan, and Saddler John A. Bailey, under the command of Sergeant Benjamin C. Criswell. It appears that McDougall himself never did go down to the river to pay his last respects to the slain junior officer of his company. As a result of the samaritan act of these five men, two were recommended for the Medal of Honor, Ryan and Criswell, while only one, Criswell, actually received this coveted medal. For testimony on the dead and burial of Hodgson, see Richard G. Hardorff, *The Custer Battle Casualties* (El Segundo, CA: Upton and Sons, 1989), pp. 127-31. See also A.L. DeVoto's account, "Description of Reno's Fight," appended to his letter to W.M. Camp, dated 10/1/1917, LBHNM, and the John A. Bailey interview in Liddic and Harbaugh, *Camp on Custer: Transcribing the Custer Myth* (Spokane: Arthur H. Clark Company, 1995), pp. 81-82.

[8](Camp note:) A commissioned officer of the Seventh Cavalry

who was present at the battle of the Little Bighorn, and who was not unfriendly to Reno, has told me that about the time of the arrival of the pack train, Maj. Reno saluted him by holding up a flask of whiskey and that his remarks and manners were silly. Said officer stated that the incident remained distinct in his memory for one reason because the bottle was then half full and Reno did not invite him to take a drink of it. (Camp MSS, transcripts, p. 103, IU Library, IN.)

[9]We quote here from Camp's interview with DeRudio, in Hammer, *Custer in '76*, p. 83: DeRudio says that in the spring of 1876 he was promoted to First Lieut., and being in Company E, he should have been put in command of it, as was customary. However, Custer put A.E. Smith in command. Smith belonged to Company A, and Custer had DeRudio and Smith change places. Smith was a favorite of Custer, and for this DeRudio never quite forgave Custer. DeRudio did not enjoy serving in Co. A under Moylan.

[10]Captain Myles Moylan. Having served since 1857, Moylan was a veteran who had come up through the ranks of the enlisted men, and who for that reason was shunned by most of the military graduates in the regiment.

[11](E.G. Mathey to Camp, 4/13/1910, BYU:)At the time I was riding Comanche the horse belonged to the Government, and if Col. Keogh ever bought the horse I never heard of it, and I believe the horse belonged to the U.S. at the time Col. Keogh was killed. Comanche was received, with other horses, when the 7th Cav. was in camp, near Ft. Dodge, Kansas, preparing for the Washita Campaign. I think it was sometime during Sept., or Oct. 1868, [and] the horse was four (4) years old that spring, so that he was about 12 years old when Col. Keogh was killed, and perhaps not many persons ever heard anything about Comanche's age.

(Camp note:) DeRudio says Comanche was a troop horse and did not belong to Keogh. Says I Co. adopted him because Keogh happened to be riding him the day of the battle. (Camp MSS, transcripts, p. 100, IU Library, IN.)

INTERVIEW WITH FOUR WOMAN

[Standing Rock Indian Reservation,] May 21, 1909[1]

Weeya-to-pa-we, means four woman [Lakota name of] Mrs. H.H. Welsh, Hunkpapa, 42 years old. Pazeezla-wak-pa is Sioux name for Greasy Grass Creek. [She] was a little girl, bathing in the river, when two scouts reported soldiers coming. Left village and when some distance away saw soldiers on top of the hills across, going north (Custer). Then some of the squaws, old men and children ran away from the village and did not come back. Went and stayed there, but some of the men went back to the village and brought more horses and food and tepees.

Being in [the river] bathing about noon, two Indian scouts came in and reported soldiers coming. Got out of the creek in a hurry and was much exited and ran from village. Hurried away with old men and squaws, with horses. Before [they] got horses in and got ready to start, soldiers had come. After this [she] saw soldiers on bluffs across the river, going north—that is, when leaving the village she saw Custer on the bluffs across the river.

[She] had a hard time leaving the village. While saddling up horses, firing had begun. Horses became frightened and hard to hold and mount. When [we] got some distance from the village [we] stopped and messengers brought word, and some wounded Indians were also brought out to us. We stopped there and did not go any farther. This was some miles away, but still in sight of the village. [There was] much excitement among those fleeing as travois were coming loose, etc. Some children on horses with mothers, some horses carrying children, and some on travois. Some Ogalalla, some Sans Arc, [and some] Minneconjou, etc. children and women also fled with the party.

After we had stopped, some old men went back to the village for tepees. We went out west over the hills. We did not travel all afternoon before stopping. At first she said she thought [they] went about 20 miles, but later said [they] did not move all 20 miles before stopping. From where we stopped we could see the village...

She thinks Minneconjou tepees were next to Hunkpapas. Sitting Bull's father was a full blood Hunkpapa and his mother a Sans Arc. Mrs. Welsh is a niece of Sitting Bull, her mother being a sister of Sitting Bull. Her father was a Minneconjou subchief. She thinks there must have been a party of perhaps 300 old men, women and children that left the village when the fighting started, of which party she was a member. Hunkpapas were encamped in a circle of tepees, the circumference of which was about 1000 ft in diameter, as she pointed out to me. One Bull is my brother.[2] Jesse Pleets interpreted Mrs. Welsh.

When two scouts reported soldiers [were] coming, men ran down to the river and told the children to hurry up to the tepees, as the women and children would have to be sent away. At first we regarded it as a joke, but the messenger assured us that two Sioux had come in and reported soldiers coming, etc.

---

[1]Camp Manuscript, field notes, box 3, BYU. Born in 1867, *Winyan Topa Win*, or, Mrs. Four Woman, was the daughter of Pretty Feather Woman and Makes Room, a Minneconjou band chief. Four Woman was married to Herbert H. Welsh, a Lakota graduate of Hampton Institute, who was known among the Hunkpapas as *Mahpiya Mato* 'Bear Cloud.' In Lakota society, the number four is regarded as a sacred number.

[2]One Bull was a brother of White Bull. Their joint interview appears hereafter.

Interview with Young Hawk

[Fort Berthold Indian Reservation. No date][1]

Indian scouts in timber: Forked Horn, Goose, Young Hawk, Foolish Bear, Bobtail Bull, Bloody Knife, Little Brave, White Swan, Half Yellow Face, Billy Cross, Watokshu.[2] Bobtail Bull headed off by Sioux and killed near timber. Little Brave was killed where some trees were chopped down near the river, and to the left of the line of retreat. Billy Cross got out before Young Hawk, and when we got on the hill Billy met us and told how he got out of the bottoms.

Custer had repeatedly ordered that in case we got scattered we should rally on the pack train where the ammunition was, and this was the reason the Rees made for the pack train. When I got to the top of the hill an officer with a handkerchief tied around his head (Reno) shook hands with me and told me where I could get another horse, as mine had been killed.[3]

Says Baker[4] was surely in the fight on June 25, and had his horse killed, but I think he means Herendeen.[5] Bear's Eyes, Owl, and Black Porcupine went back with messages from Powder River. Young Hawk, One Feather, and Forked Horn out scouting while Crows went to Crow's Nest night of June 24. Scouts at Crow's Nest were Bobtail Bull, Bloody Knife, Black Fox, White Calf (Red Star)[6] and Bull. Red Star and Bull took message to Custer from Crow's Nest (first party sent). Bloody Knife, Bobtaill Bull and one of the Crows second party sent.

About Left Hand. Young Hawk says he was a Sioux, and when his [enlistment] time expired he left and joined the Sioux. The Rees afterward found his horse in the Sioux village, and Left Hand was one of the dead Indians left by the Sioux in the village.[7]

On the expedition we went swimming, and while we were doing this the older of the two Jackson boys came along with a revolver and said: "Look here. See what I will do when we meet the Sioux." He then fired all the shots of his revolver, when the Officer-of-the-Day came running out and put him under arrest. For punishment he was made to stand with one foot at a time on a barrel and the other on the ground, all day.

---

[1]Camp MSS, field notes, unclassified envelope 77, IU Library, IN. Born in 1855 near Mannhaven, North Dakota, the Arikara Young Hawk was the son of Red Corn Silk Woman and Horn in Front. He enlisted in 1874 as a US Indian Scout and was present in both the valley and hilltop fights. He passed away on January 16, 1915, at Elbowoods, North Dakota. For additional interviews with Young Havk, see Hammer, *Custer in '76,* pp. 192-94, and also Orin G. Libby, *The Arikara Narrative of the Campaign against Hostile Dakotas, June 1876* (New York: Sol Lewis, 1973), pp. 48-52, 69-71, 93-115.

The following extract sheds some interesting light on the origin of the Libby interviews, which were conducted in August 1912, one month after Camp had completed his fieldwork among the Rees. (Camp to Gen. E.S. Godfrey, 1/4/1918, Godfrey Papers, Library of Congress:) At that time [1912] Dr. Libby had never seen any of the old Ree scouts, and there were not, therefore, any statements from or interviews with them on file at the historical society. It was my trips to see the old Ree scouts, five years in succession [1909-1913], that put into the head of Dr. Libby the idea of visiting them himself.

I have never met Dr. Libby personally, but called several times on his collaborator, Mr. Fish [NDHS curator], and Fish told me, after finding what I had been doing among the Rees, that he was going to suggest to Libby that the latter visit them as I had done. Upon his first visit to the Rees he found out that I was well known among them, whereupon he took occasion to inform them that he had charge of all historical matters pertaining to the State of North Dakota, and advised them not to again be interviewed by any one on historical matters unless the person should have credentials from himself, as secretary of the State Historical Society. I was told this by several Indians and white people [in 1913] who heard Dr. Libby so advise the old scouts. Having already finished my work among the Rees before Dr. Libby ever saw them, I was not greatly disturbed over his attempt to corral their historical information.

In my interviews with nine of the eleven Ree scouts whom I met I found two or three of them to be notorious liars concerning their experiences at the battle of the Little Bighorn. Evidently they thought I was believing all they said. When Libby's interviews are printed, I shall be interested to see how much weight he will give to certain chaps who thought they were "stuffing" me.

[2] *Watoksu,* a Siouan word meaning "ring," was an abbreviated appellation for *Watoksu Mahpiya* 'Ring Cloud,' whose interview follows hereafter.

[3] This may have been Lt. Charles A. Varnum because it was he who, according to Lt. Winfield S. Edgerly, had tied a white handkerchied *around* his head, while Major Reno wore one *on* his head.

[4] William Baker, a mixed-blood scout, whose interview follows hereafter.

[5] George Herendeen, a civilian scout.

[6] Also known as Strikes the Bear and White Calf, Red Star related his experiences of the Sioux expedition to Libby in *Arikara Narrative,* pp. 57-63, 66-69, 71-73, 118-21.

[7] The body of the Lakota named *Catka* 'Left Hand' was found laying on a tanned buffalo robe in the deserted Indian village. The remains were dressed in a white burial shirt, of which the shoulders were painted red, while the forehead of the deceased bore the sacred red symbol of a warrior society.

Interview with Strikes Two
[Fort Berthold Indian Reservation. No date][1]

He was 29 years old at time of battle. At Crow's Nest early on June 25: Charlie Reynolds, Mitch Bouyer,[2] five Crows, and five Rees: White Calf (Red Star), Bull, and

Forked Horn. Don't remember the other two [Rees]. I
was left at pack train. Bobtail Bull and Bloody Knife not
at Crow's Nest. Says White Calf enlisted same time as
myself.

Red Star, Boy Chief[3] and Strikes Two captured 27
horses and 2 mules. We had made a break for a drove of
horses on our way down from Ford A, but the Sioux
were too quick and got them away, but the above 29
appeared to break away from the herd and we three got
them. [We were] in the timber before soldiers got to timber, and we ran the ponies up the bluffs and there we
passed Custer going north along the bluffs, and a few of
Custer's soldiers, taking us for Sioux, fired at us and hit
Boy Chief's horse in the jaw. We kept waving our hats to
let them know we were Rees. Custer kept going right on
and soon got out of our sight.

We were joined by others soon and there were eight of
us with the captured Sioux horses: Little Sioux,[4] One
Feather, Bull in Water, one of the Sioux [scouts], Red
Star, Soldier (Kannoch),[5] Boy Chief, and Strikes Two.
We took the horses back until we met the pack train
coming, and then left them there with holders.

In the morning of June 25, after we knew that Sioux
were in valley, Mitch Bouyer told us that he said to
Custer: ["] Why not wait a day until Gibbon cooperates
as there are too many Sioux. ["] Custer said: ["]There
are no more than I handled in another battle.["] Custer
called the officers together and had a council and after
this told us he was going to charge the camp, and he
wanted us scouts, at the proper time, to go ahead and get
the Sioux horses and run them up back of the pack train
and stay there, because if we were in front of the soldiers
they would take us for Sioux and fire on us. ["]Those
soldiers,["] said Custer, ["]would not be able to tell the

difference between a Sioux and a Ree.["] He said we could have all the horses we would capture.

When we got down near the river Custer said: ["]Why don't you go ahead? What are you waiting for?["] Then Strikes Two, Forked Horn, Bobtail Bull, Little Brave, Foolish Red Bear, Watokchu and another Sioux crossed the river and made a rush for the horses, but the Sioux got them away. Later we got some of the horses as stated above. Watokchu was in fight in bottom. Good Elk in fight in bottom. Foolish Red Bear and Goose also in fight in bottom.

Left horses with holders and came back to bluffs, and Cross said we ought to get horses farther away so as to make a sure thing of them. Bush, One Feather, Good Face, Red Star, and Little Crow started back toward Powder with these horses. Rest of us stopped with Reno. Nine of us returned from horses and stayed with Reno. We then counted ourselves and concluded that eight of us had been killed, including Young Hawk, Goose, Foolish Red Bear,[6] and Forked Horn whom we at that time did not know were with the soldiers.

We were joined by Billy Cross and went to river to water the horses, and while there Reno was surrounded by the Sioux. We ascended the bluffs and waited, and seeing Reno beseiged and it getting dark (could see the flash of guns), Stab said: ["]We cannot go to the soldiers. Let us go to Powder River.["] We camped half way. (Did not appear to know Baker at all.) The Rees with the horses were way up ahead and we did not overtake them that night. [However,] the Sioux had chased them and had retaken the horses.

The reason the few Rees started out early with the horses was that we thought that to make a sure thing of them, we had better get them to Powder River. Custer had told us to get the herd and get it in rear of the pack train, and we could have all the horses we could capture, which was to us a great incentive to capture all we could.

————————

[1]Camp MSS, field notes, unclassified envelope 77, IU Library, IN. Born at Ft. Clark in 1847, Strikes Two was the son of Young Woman Village and Arikara Chief. He enlisted in 1873, and served in 1874 and 1876. He was a member of the party which captured Sioux ponies in the valley. He did not participate in the hilltop fight. He died on September 8, 1922, at Elbowood, North Dakota. Other interviews with Strikes Two may be found in Hammer, *Custer in '76*, pp. 183-86, and in Libby, *Arikara Narrative*, pp. 118-19.

[2](Camp note:) Antoine Bouyer, July 13, 1912, says Mitch Bouyer's name was Michel Bouyer. Mitch's father [Vital] was a full blood Frenchman who was killed by Indians while trapping. Mother of Mitch was a full blood Santee Sioux. (Camp MSS, transcript, p. 53, IU Library, IN.) Mitch Bouyer was a stepbrother of William Garnett.

[3]The experiences of Boy Chief are recorded in Libby, *Arikara Narrative*, pp. 53-55, 118-19.

[4]For interviews with Little Sioux, see Hammer, *Custer in '76*, pp. 180-82, and Libby, *Arikara Narrative*, pp. 149-57.

[5]Soldier's experiences are related in Hammer, *Custer in '76*, pp. 187-91, and Libby, *Arikara Narrative*, pp. 46-48, 55-57, 115-18.

[6]Red Bear's account may be found in Hammer, *Custer in '76*, p. 194, and Libby, *Arikara Narrative*, pp. 52-53, 63-66, 121-35.

————————

INTERVIEW WITH YOUNG HAWK AND STRIKES TWO
[Fort Berthold Indian Reservation, August 7, 1910][1]

Was Billy Cross with the party who captured ponies or in Reno's retreat? In Reno's retreat. Did they see anything of White Swan's fight? Yes, it was during the retreat of the Rees. Was Young Hawk left in the timber mounted or dismounted and how did he get out? Mounted. Did those who captured ponies see anything of Custer and his five companies when they ascended the bluffs or before? Yes, passed near him and were shot at by a few soldiers. They must therefore have come up just after Knipe[2] left. How long before battle began did Rees capture Sioux horses?[3] Quite a while. How far was it from the place [where they] ran them up the bluffs to the Reno corral? Just about where Reno retreated up, says Strikes Two. Who was the brother of Boy Chief? Good Elk. It is an error to say that the Rees, who passed the pack train, had then started for Powder River. The Rees who captured the ponies ran them up the valley a few miles to get them out of sight and left them with holders.

Both Young Hawk and Strikes Two said there were two Jacksons and two white scouts. Neither of them seemed to remember that there were three half-breeds. Young Hawk said the two white men were called Ieska[4] and Choka Wo.[5] Ieska was thought by Young Hawk to be Billy Cross and Choka Wo to be Baker. Said Choka Wo's horse was killed and that Choka Wo was left in the timber and he got a Sioux horse. This may have been Cross. Strikes Two was more definite and said that one of the two white men was killed (Charley Reynolds) and the other (Choka Wo) went to Powder River, with the Rees. Choka Wo must therefore have been Cross. Neither of them appears to remember Baker. Strikes Two says Choka Wo is the one who came down the hill with the Rees to water the horses and got cut off from Reno by the Sioux.[6]

---

[1]Camp MSS, field notes, unclassified envelope 77, IU Library, IN.

[2]Sergeant Daniel A. Knipe (Kanipe), who was detached from Custer's column, just north of Reno Hill, with a message to hurry up the pack train.

[3](Camp note: Boy Chief says Rees who captured horses were: Forked Horn, Boy Chief, Strikes Two, Bull in Water, Little Sioux, Red Star, The Whole Buffalo, One Feather, Soldier, Stab, Little Crow, Red Wolf, [and] Strikes the Lodge. (Camp MSS, transcripts, p. 468, IU Library, IN.)

[4]Ieska, or rather *Iyeska,* is a Siouan word derived from *iye* 'to speak' and *ska* 'white.' The Lakotas applies this term to the mixed-blood children born from marriages between Indians and whites. In a broader sense, the word means "interpreter," since many of the mixed-bloods rendered services as translators.

[5]Choka Wo is the phonetical spelling of the Siouan word *Cank-abu,* derived from *kabubu* 'to drum,' and means "drummer." This was the Lakota appellation for William Baker, alias William Bailey, whose interview follows hereafter.

[6](Inquiry Rees [in 1913]:) What white and half breed scouts were with Rees and who went back to Powder River? Only Billy Cross. What scouts (white or half breed) at Little Bighorn? Bill Baker was there says Young Hawk. Ditto says Running Wolf. (Camp MSS, transcripts, p. 406, IU Library, IN.)

INTERVIEW WITH RING CLOUD

[Standing Rock Indian Reservation,] May 21, 1909[1]

Watokshu Mahpia (Ring Cloud). Adam Carrier [is] my English name, 73 years old. Harry McLaughlin interpreter. Was at Grand River Agency and about four years before the battle went up to see Custer and Custer asked him to be a scout... Accordingly, my brother and I enlisted. My brother's name was Appearing Bear (Matokia Napa).[2] Rees did not know country well, and so Custer thought it would be well to take me along. Twenty-eight Indian Scouts [with Custer], including Crows and Rees and we two Blackfeet Sioux. Bloody

Knife was half Ree and half Sioux. There were also two Jackson brothers and "Scolla" Billy Cross and the Crow interpreter (Bouyer)—all half breeds. Reason he [Ring Cloud] went with Custer [was because] his father and mother were dead and wanted to earn money.

On way back to Powder River nearly starved. Got nothing to eat until got to Powder River. Slept twice on way back. Sundance Creek known to him as the creek now called Benteen Creek. Scouts went down ahead of Reno on advance from Ford A. Some of them captured Sioux ponies and mules and drove them to Powder River. Some recrossed in retreat near Ford A and others below were Rees did. Says two Jacksons[3] and Billy Cross in Reno's valley fight. Two half breed scouts did not go back with them but followed them.

F.F. Gerard called Fast Bull. [I] knew him and was with Varnum at Crow's Nest at daylight 6/25, and went back to Custer with message from Varnum. Slept twice on way back to Powder. Passed pack train and told them [Reno's] soldiers scattered and running, but officer said [he] did not believe it ...

---

[1]Camp Manuscript, field notes, box 3, BYU. *Watoksu Mahpiya* 'Ring Cloud' was a Blackfoot Lakota who was born in 1836. He was a veteran U.S. Indian Scout who signed his first enlistment in 1871.

[2]*Mato Kinapa* 'Appearing Bear' was the older brother of Ring Cloud. Born in 1827, Appearing Bear signed his tenth enlistment on February 3, 1876, at Ft. Lincoln.

[3]Born on August 27, 1856, William "Billy" Jackson was the younger brother of Bob Jackson. He enlisted as a scout at Ft. Lincoln on December 10, 1874, and served continuously through December of 1876. He reenlisted at Cantonment Tongue River in the spring of 1877, and served intermittently at several Montana army posts for the next several years. Billy Jackson was left behind in the timber upon Reno's retreat from the valley.

INTERVIEW WITH RING CLOUD
Standing Rock, May 30, 1909[1]

Harry McLaughlin interpreter. Watokshu, Ring Cloud, 73 years old, brother of Matokia Napa, Comes the Bear. Brother with him on Little Bighorn. [There were] four Sioux.[2] Two went back before crossing the divide.[3] Seize the Buffalo and White Cloud were the two other Sioux. [There was] a Ree named Bear in the Timber. Three Rees killed: Bloody Knife, Bobtail Bull, and Little Soldier. Knew Stab, but Stab not killed. Big battle, big dust and wind blowing and could not see who killed. Was on the divide early 6/25 and could see ponies. Gerard called Fast Bull... Isaiah called Black Hawk. Has a son at Ft. Yates named Baptiste Black Hawk.[4]

Part of the Indian scouts went for the Sioux pony herd over in the hills, and part went to the edge of timber and retreated direct across the river and waited until pack train came up. Then all but two Rees went to the river to get a drink, and while gone, the troops were surrounded by the Sioux and we were cut off and went back on the trail to Powder River. Billy Cross was with us.

In early a.m. [June 25th], in a talk with Custer, told Custer: ["]Too many Sioux, too many to surround them.["] Custer thought he could surround the Sioux and defeat them. In Reno valley fight I shot a Sioux with buckskin coat. He shot at me and missed me, and then I shot and knocked him off his horse, but I did not wait to see if he had been killed.

---

[1]Camp Manuscript, field notes, box 3, BYU.

[2]The following Lakota scouts were present at the Little Bighorn: Ring Cloud 'Watoksu Mahpiya' (possibly reenlisted on 2/3/1876), Appearing Bear 'Mato Kinapa' (10th enlistment on 2/3/1876), White Cloud 'Mahpiya Ska' (3rd enlistment on 5/14/1876), and Seize the Buffalo 'Tatanka Iyapaya' (2nd enlistment on 3/31/1876).

[3]Some of the Lakota names listed in the *Arikara Narrative* are impossible to be reconciled with the names recorded on the muster rolls of June 1876. In part this problem is due to the inability of interpreters to translate the finer nuances of Lakota into English. Moreover, each interpreter pronounced and spelled Lakota words according to his perception of names. I should also point out that intertribal marriages between the Sioux and Rees were not uncommon, which may have been the case with the Lakota scouts. If so, the possibility exists that some of the Lakota names in the *Arikara Narrative* were Ree interpretations. This, coupled with the possibility that the Lakota scouts may have been known by nicknames— either in Ree or Lakota language, or both—has led to considerable confusion.

The names of the two Lakota scouts who did not cross the divide were Left Hand and Shield. I base my identification on the evidence contained in Walter Camp's list in Hammer, *Custer in '76*, p. 283. Of the five discharged scouts, the enlistment of two, Broken Penis and Cards, expired before the expedition started. Of the remaining three, Sticking Out was identified as a Ree, which leaves us with Left Hand and Shield. Left Hand (discharged on 6/9/1876) was identified by Young Hawk as a Lakota, while Shield (discharged on 6/11/1876) was known by the equivalent name of *Waha Canka,* which is clearly Lakota.

[4]Subsequent inquiry by Walter Camp at Ft. Yates failed to locate the son of Isaiah Dorman.

INTERVIEW WITH HAIRY MOCCASIN
[Crow Agency,] July 17 , 1910 [1]

Says that when Custer separated from Reno he took Mitch Bouyer and three Crows. No other scout, white, Indian or half breed, was taken. Says Curley left before Custer separated from Reno. He recognized Billy Cross' picture and said that he (Cross) went with Reno in the valley. Hairy Moccasin says that from the bluffs he saw

Reno's fight and retreat, and that the three Crows met the other soldiers (Benteen), who came up and joined Reno after the retreat out of the valley. Hairy Moccasin pointed out the vicinity of Ford A as the place where they met Benteen. Fenton Campbell was the interpreter. He could not interpret all of the questions I wished to ask, but the foregoing statements of Hairy Moccasin were unmistakable as he told them to me in English. He understood enough English to communicate that much.

---

[1]Camp MSS, field notes, unclassified envelope 135, IU Library, IN. Born in 1853, Hairy Moccasin was a member of the mountain division of the *Apsáalooke* Nation (People of the Large-beaked Bird), a tribal name translated erroneously as Crow Indians. He enlisted as a scout in the Seventh Infantry on April 10, 1876, and was transferred to the Seventh Cavalry on June 21. He withdrew from Custer's battalion somewhere near Weir Point. Hairy Moccasin died on October 9, 1922, at Lodgegrass, Montana. For other interviews with him, see Hammer, *Custer in '76*, pp. 176-77; Joseph K. Dixon, *The Vanishing Race* (New York: Bonanza Books, 1975), pp. 138-40; and Herbert Coffeen, *The Custer Battle Book* (New York: Carlton Press, 1964), pp. 48-49.

INTERVIEW WITH WILLIAM HEYN
[No date][1]

Says that sometime after Weir[2] went out toward Custer the whole outfit moved down the river, he [Heyn] being carried on a blanket; but [they] did not go far before [they] halted and fell back.

When he left the skirmish line there were no officers on it. He mounted up the troop and rode toward the south side of the timber. There he saw Moylan and Reno just in the edge of the timber, with cocked revolvers, ready to go out. The men straggled out and started across the flat without any particular command and no bugle being blown, officers digging spurs into their horses and every man for himself.

W. Heyn, 1st Sergt. of Troop A, says that when the men fell back from the skirmish line to the woods there were no officers on the line. When on the skirmish line the shell ejectors of his carbine would not work, and he borrowed a ramrod from Wallace[3] to get the shell out, as Wallace had a sporting rifle. When he fell back to the woods Moylan and Reno were mounted, and Trumpeter McVey,[4] of his troop, who held his horse, called to him and said: "For God's sake, Sergeant, take your horse — we're going to retreat." In the timber Heyn was shot in the knee, the bullet passing into his horse. On the way to the river Roy's[5] horse was shot, and his own horse was hit twice more, once through the neck and at the roots of his tail. Lieut. Hodgson was riding at Heyn's left side, and while crossing the river Hodgson was shot and fell off his horse into the river. Heyn's horse carried him to the top of the bluff, but he died the next morning.

Benteen got up about the same time that Reno went up the bluff. Heyn says Benteen was walking around all the time, encouraging the men, while bullets were whistling all about him, and [he] was regarded as the hero of the fight.

------

[1]Camp Manuscript, field notes, box 2, BYU. Born in 1848 in Bremen, Germany, William Heyn enlisted in the Third Cavalry in 1867, and reenlisted in 1872 in the Seventh Cavalry. After his recovery of the gunshot wound in his left knee, Sergeant Heyn was transferred to the GSAGO and discharged on April 6, 1877, upon expiration of his enlistment, as a First Sergeant of very good charac-

ter. He reenlisted in the GS in the same year and served in the Adjutant's General Office for some ten years, completing his military career with two years of service at the Headquarters of the Army. One June 25, Heyn was First Sergeant of A Company. The Camp Collection at BYU contains two of Heyn's letters.

[2] Capt. Thomas B. Weir, commanding D Company.

[3] Lt. George D. Wallace, G Company. He was assigned to Headquarters Staff on June 22, 1876, as the regimental Engineer Officer. At the request of Lt. Charles A. Varnum, his West Point classmate, Lt. Wallace was granted permission by Custer to accompany Reno's battalion into the valley, an act which saved Wallace's life.

[4] Trumpeter David McVeigh, A Company.

[5] Sergeant Stanislas Roy, A Company. His interview follows hereafter.

Interview with Thomas W. Harrison
[No date][1]

Thos. W. Harrison, D Co., says D Troop had black horses. Vincent Charley[2] was killed between the two Edgerly Peaks.[3] He was orderly for Edgerly and was with Edgerly when he came near being taken in while trying to mount his horse. Indians had got around behind them and they had to draw their revolvers and cut through on their retreat back.

When D Troop retreated they failed to rescue Charley, and when Edgerly and Harrison got away from the peak it was occupied by Indians and [it was] then too late to help Charley, who was shot through the hips and was making his way to the rear the best he could, half crawling on his feet and one hand.[4]

Says he was sure Sergeant Morton[5] was not there. Was

at Ft. Lincoln sick. Pat Golden,[6] of D Troop, was killed when men on north line charged out on command of Benteen.

---

[1]Camp Manuscript, field notes, box 3, BYU. Born in ireland in 1849, Thomas Harrison enlisted in D Company in August 1871, and was discharged on August 5, 1876, at the mouth of the Rosebud, upon expiration of service, as a Sergeant. A second interview may be found in Liddic and Harbaugh, *Camp on Custer*, pp. 97-98.

[2]Farrier Vincent Charley, D Company, whose name is listed on the monument as Chas. Vincent.

[3]D Company was routinely commanded by Lt. Winfield S. Edgerly per consent of his superior officer, Capt. Thomas B. Weir. According to Edgerly, the name of his orderly was Private Saunders, and we must therefore assume that Harrison was incorrect in his recollection. However, Edgerly was mistaken, also, because Private Richard D. Saunders, a recent recruit, had died on Custer's battlefield, he being a member of F Company. I assume, therefore, that Edgerly meant Private Charles Sanders, D Company, who had signed his third enlistment on June 26, 1872, at age 28, and who, quite probably, was the individual to whom Edgerly referred as "an old veteran." Nonetheless, Harrison did assist Edgerly, who recommended him for the Medal of Honor. Wrote Edgerly: "I had considerable difficulty in mounting my horse, and Sergeant Harrison, with great danger to himself, stopped back and wrote off with me in the rear of the company." The recommendation, which was made twice, was not endorsed by the Board of Officers and a medal was thus not awarded.

[3]Pleading not to be left behind, Vincent Charley was told by Lt. Edgerly to seek safety in a washout and to lay quiet until he (Edgerly) could get help to rescue him. After the battle Charley's remains were found some 250 yards south of Weir Point. According to Edgerly, who viewed the remains, the body had a stick rammed down the throat, suggesting that the unfortunate man had been subjected to torture.

The abandonment of Charley had a profound impact on Edgerly who was troubled by this incident the rest of his life. In a letter to his wife, dated 7/4/1876, Edgerly disclosed: "He [Capt. Weir] said orders had been given to fall back and we must obey them. That was the one thing I regretted more than any other thing that happened to me, for I had promised that wounded man I would get him out and wasn't able to raise a [finger] for him." This feeling of guilt, linked, possibly, with resentment toward Weir, came to expression once again at the Reno Court of Inquiry in 1879. Edgerly's statement reveals that he had pleaded with Weir to rescue Charley; that he (Edgerly) had given his word as an officer to the wounded man that he would come back to save him; but that his pleadings with Weir had fallen on deaf ears. Thirty years later, this whole matter was still fresh in Edgerly's mind when he was interviewed by Walter Camp.

The death of Vincent Charley was of very little consequence when measured against the casualty totals sustained on other parts of the field. Yet, I cannot escape the thought that the abandonment of this one man presents itself as a pathetic story of trust and betrayal. To those students who condemn Reno for abandoning his wounded and who champion Weir for his quick resolve to go to Custer's aid, I suggest they take another look at Weir's involvement in the abandonment of Vincent Charley. I find Weir's conduct in that matter deplorable.

[5]Sergeant Thomas Morton, D Company, who was on sick leave at Ft. Lincoln Hospital since May 15, 1876.

[6]Private Pat M. Golden, D Company. He was killed on June 26.

Interview with John Rafter
[No date][1]

Says [he] was digging pits with knives, forks and spoons. Mrs. Rafter says there were twenty-six widows at Ft. Lincoln as a result of the battle of the Little Bighorn. Garlick married the widow of Trumpeter Dose of G Co.[2] Mrs. Rafter was the widow of Francis T. Hughes of L Co.

Rafter says Weston Harrington's body of L Co. was found between Custer and the deep gully. The body was not mutilated and a blanket was thrown over him. He was known among the Sioux before he was enlisted and it was thought that some of them recognized him and protected his body in this way.

Rafter remembers talk of two men who straggled back from [Custer's] five companies to the pack train before it got to the river. Says he (Rafter) had charge of the detail when carrying Mike Madden when he fell off the stretcher in being carried to the steamer on the night of June 26. Says stretchers between mules did not work well. Rafter says he helped carry Mike Madden up the bluff after he was wounded in going for water on June 26.[3] Says Foley and Rott and himself went for water.[4]

---

[1]Camp MSS, field notes, Little Bighorn, Battle of 1876, III, box 2, IU Library, IN. Born in New York in 1851, Sergeant John Rafter enlisted in K Company on January 20, 1872, and served until January 25, 1882, when he was discharged at Ft. Lincoln, upon expiration of his service, as a Private of fair character, having been demoted during his second term.

[2]Edward Garlick, First Sergeant of G Company, married Elizabeth Hahn Dose on November 22, 1876, at Bismarck, Dakota. She was the widow of Trumpeter Henry C. Dose, G Company, who was Custer's orderly on June 25.

[3]Saddler Michael P. Madden, K Company, sustained a double fracture from a gunshot below the right knee, which necessitated the amputation of his leg on June 26. He was promoted on the same day to Sergeant for his gallantry on the battlefield.

(Camp note:) Inquiry Godfrey: Why was Mike Madden not awarded a medal for going for water? Godfrey says he recommended him, but no medal was awarded. (Camp Manuscript, transcript, p. 184, BYU.)

[4]Private John Foley and Sergeant Louis Rott, both of K Company.

(We quote here from a letter by E.S. Godfrey to Walter Camp, 5/14/1923, BYU:) I have always understood that all those who volunteered to get water were recommended for the Medal of Honor. I know I did. Those recommendations were referred to a Board of

Officers of which, I think, Maj. Merrill was president when the regiment was in camp at Sturgis, near Bear Butte, Black Hills, in 1878. I have an indirect recollection that the Board turned down all except those who made the *first* and perhaps the *second* "rush" for water, and only those who were then (1878) in the service...

INTERVIEW WITH STANISLAS ROY
[September 16, 1910][1]

Indian killed near H Co. line had a large belt full of ammunition.[2] Says Custer's route up the Rosebud most of the way was on the west side. Says camp at 5 p.m. on June 24 was on a flat on the east side.

Says that one of the tepees in the village in which dead Indians were found was opposite to Crazy Horse Coulee.[3] This tepee was burned up with the bodies.

Says Benteen had heel of [his] boot shot off and foot was stunned so that he walked lame for a few days. On Sept. 16, 1910, Roy says positively that after identifying Foley he crossed [a] ravine and in about 200 yards came upon the body of Sergeant Butler of L Co.[4]

Roy says there were a number of dead cavalry horses near the men A Co. buried, between Custer and the ravine. I, myself, saw the bones of a good many [in 1903]. This contradicts what some have said to prove that the men who left the ridge were all dismounted.[5]

---

[1]Camp MSS, field notes, box 2 and unclassified envelope 135, IU Library, IN. Stanislas Roy was born in France in 1847, and enlisted in H Company on January 19, 1870. Upon reenlistment he was transferred to A Company, and was discharged on January 18,

1880, at Ft. Meade, Dakota, upon expiration of service, as a Sergeant of excellent character. He was awarded the Medal of Honor in 1878, for having "brought water to the wounded at great danger to life and under a great and most galling fire of the enemy." Sergeant Roy served six additional terms, all in A Company, retiring from service on June 30, 1901, with the rank of Color Sergeant. He passed away on February 10, 1913, and was buried in Greenlawn Cemetery, Government Lot, Grave 183, at Columbus Barracks, Ohio. Roy's lengthy correspondence with Walter Camp (1909-1912) is housed at BYU. In August of 1909, Roy accompanied Daniel A. Knipe and Walter Camp to Custer's battlefield where he was interviewed, the results published in Hammer, *Custer in '76*, pp. 111-17. For another account of Roy's experiences at the Little Bighorn, see Adolph Roenigk, *Pioneer History of Kansas* (No place: Published by Adolph Roenigk, 1933), pp. 288-95.

[2]The name of this Lakota was *Canku Hanska* 'Long Road,' a young Sans Arc who was slain on June 26. For an account of his death, see Richard G. Hardorff, *Hokahey! A Good Day to Die! The Indian Casualties of the Custer Fight.* (Spokane: Arthur H. Clark Company, 1993), pp. 87-91.

[3]Crazy Horse Coulee is presently known as Deep Ravine. Camp's use of nomenclature was based on information obtained from Indian combatants who identified Deep Ravine as the coulee through which Crazy Horse ascended Custer's battlefield.

[4]Corporal John Foley, C Company, and Sergeant James Butler, L Company.

(Extract of a questionnaire, appended to Roy's letter to Camp, 3/4/1909, BYU:) I knew Sergt. Butler well. He was a heavy set man [who] wore side-whiskers and had a bald head. There is no doubt he tried to make Reno's command. There was also a man found on the trail that got farther south than Butler. His name was Foley, belonging to C Troop. He was the first man [found] dead on the trail the morning of the 28th...

(Roy to Camp, 9/13/1909, BYU:) Foley's body lay back of the Dry Creek, between Dry Creek and next coulee north, and Butler north of coulee. The distance I cannot estimate, but [it was] a long ways from the reservation fence or [where] first bunch of dead was found north of the fence.

(Camp notes:) 800 feet from river to top of slope of little hill on which Foley found. Edge of rise of ground on which Foley was found is 800 feet from river. Foley's body was found about 1100 feet from river.

The nearest dead soldier to Ford B in the direction of Custer was on second little hill north of first ravine beyond B - 6/10 mile beyond B. There were no more bodies in this vicinity. This must have been Butler. Possibly they did not find Foley, as they naturally would not, in going to Butler direct from Ford B [see Camp's map].

In my opinion Butler may have been killed on Custer's retreat up from the river as his body lay right on the trail. Foley lay back some 800 feet from the trail and may have been the one trying to escape and was pursued a mile and who shot himself. His reason for shooting himself may have been that he was wounded and began to feel his strength fail. Foley may also have been sent as a messenger late in the battle, as he was in Tom Custer's company and may have been sent by that officer the same as Knipe was sent. (Camp MSS, transcripts, p. 559, IU Library, IN.)

Based on evidence provided by Roy and other contemporary sources, it appears that Butler was found on a rise just south of Deep Coulee, some 600 yards northeast from where the present blacktop road cuts across the ravine. Butler's kill site was identified by Gen. Godfrey in 1916, and although a stone marker was placed the following year, it was erected at a location which was some 300 yards west from the site marked by Godfrey. By 1949, Superintendent Edward S. Luce had become convinced that Butler's marker stood at the wrong location. Guided by the 1891 USGS topographical map, Luce hauled the stone some 1100 feet east and placed it at its present location. Ironically, the site elected by Luce is not the site marked by Godfrey who staked Butler's kill site some 125 yards southwest of the present marker location.

In 1904, a rotted boot, containing a decomposed foot, was found in Deep Coulee, in the area where Butler was slain. Examination of the rotted leather disclosed the presence of initials which were thought to read "JD." However, it is quite possible that the faded letters may have spelled "JB," which, if indeed the case, provides us with yet another clue to the probable location of James Butler's kill site.

I should also mention that a horse skeleton was discovered in the same area staked by Godfrey. This find corroborates the statement by Trumpeter Martin who claims that Butler was found with his

dead horse near him. Martin's observation receives further cre-
dence from Walter Camp who saw the bones of a number of horses
lying between Butler's kill site and Calhoun Ridge as late as 1903.

[5](Camp note:) Inquire particularly about the last break. Were
there any [men on] horses, etc.? Yes, 9 says One Elk. (Camp MSS,
transcripts, p. 60, IU Library, IN.)

Interview with William J. Bailey
October 8, 1910[1]

[He] was an enlisted man in 17th Inf in Yellowstone
expedition in 1873. Says the Rees called him Chakaboo,
which means drummer.[2] Says he was with the men on
the skirmish line and retreated out of the valley with
Reno and the command. His horse was shot down on
east side of the river and he caught the horse of a soldier
who had been killed and rode up on the bluff.[3] Says on
Reno Hill on evening of 6/25 he was lying beside a man
who was shot in the head.

Says that on the morning of 6/27 he was sent with
Young Hawk to go with a message for medicine.[4] In
Medicine Tail Coulee they came across two dead bodies
where I have location of Foley and Butler. Soon after this
Bradley[5] and two or three scouts came along.

Never heard that Left Hand went with Sioux after his
[enlistment] time expired. Identified my picture of
Goose.[6] Says Rees retreated out of bottom after Reno's
command did.

---

[1]Camp MSS, field notes, box 4, BYU. Born in Virginia on April
24, 1850, William James Bailey served in the Civil War as a drummer boy with the Union Army. In 1869 he enlisted with the Seven-

teenth Infantry under the assumed name of William Baker and was a member of the Yellowstone Expedition of 1873. He was on detached service with the Seventeenth Cavalry in 1874 and served as an Indian Interpreter during the Black Hills Expedition. Bailey was honorably discharged at Fort Abercrombie, Dakota Territory, in October 1874, with the rank of musician. After his discharge he was employed by the Quartermaster as an Indian Interpreter, but in May 1876, he reenlisted for a six-month term as a private with Varnum's detachment of Indian Scouts. Bailey was present in both the Valley and hilltop fights and remained with the troops till the end of of the expedition. Bailey's marriage to a Mandan woman named Sand Snake resulted in the birth of his only son, James Baker, who died on the Fort Berthold Indian Reservation, North Dakota, on December 7, 1953. After the death of his Mandan wife, Bailey moved to Montana where he married a Piegan woman on the Blackfoot Reservation in 1890. From this brief union a daughter was born, Mary Baker, who died at Great Falls, Montana, on February 19, 1947. Bailey left Montana in 1902 and eventually settled in St. Cloud, Florida, where he died on October 14, 1933. He was buried in Arlington National Cemetery in Washington, Section 13, Grave Site 81-4. The Camp Collection at BYU contains three letters by Bailey.

[2]Choko Wo, Chakowo, and Chakaboo are all phonetical variants of the Siouan word *cankabu* 'drummer.' The origin of the name is confirmed by the Rees who stated that the Sioux scouts addressed Bailey by the name of Drummer, and that he spoke Lakota.

[3](Camp note :) In a claim dated Oct. 14, 1903, Baker states: "My horse was shot under me in June 1876, while riding him and while under the command of Major Reno near the Custer Massacre during the LBH expedition." On Feb. 24, 1903, he swore to this before a notary. His claim for $200 was disallowed because [it was] not presented before Jan 9, 1894, being thereby barred by limitation of statute. (Camp Manuscript, transcript, p. 321, BYU.)

[4]Questioned by Walter Camp on this matter, the Rees stated that Young Hawk and Forked Horn carried the message, and not Bailey. However, Bailey did accompany the Rees during the morning of June 27, when they were assigned to Capt. Benteen and H Company to commence the preliminary task of identification of the slain officers on Custer's battlefield. According to Young Hawk, among those present was a man who the Sioux scouts called Jack Drum Beater, which could only have been William J. Bailey.

[5]Lt. James H. Bradley, Seventh Infantry, who commanded a mounted detachment of twelve infantry scouts.

[6]Goose was a Ree scout who sustained a serious gunshot wound to the right hand during the valley fight.

INTERVIEW WITH JOHN C. CREIGHTON
[No date][1]

Says that on Reno Hill Co. K was to right of M and left of G. Creighton, Bresnahan[2] and Madden went for water. Clear[3] killed on east side of Little Bighorn just at foot of bluff about where Bill Meyer fell.[4] Vincent Charley was killed between the two peaks. McIntosh[5] was a Cherokee Indian. Isaiah[6] was killed right near Charley Reynolds. About note in Cooke's[7] hand. Logue[8] saw Nowlan take the note from a soldier who took it out of Cooke's hand. Creighton says Loque often told of it. Bulldog "Red"[9] liked by soldiers and fondled as an old veteran after the battle of Little Bighorn. Creighton says Vickory[10] in ravine between Calhoun and Keogh. Lieut. Reilly[11] was not mutilated. Graham[12] of L Troop lay on line between Calhoun and Keogh.

Indians in soldier clothes and in company formation probably [attempted] to decoy some of Gibbon's soldiers away. DeWitt Winney[13] killed on right of K Co.'s line. Found sitting dead in a rifle pit with gun in hand across his lap. Heard of Nathan Short's white hat with "C7th" marked on it. Says he recognized Sgt. Finley[14] where I have it marked. Thinks Sgt. Fehler[15] of A Co. left in the brush…

---

[1]Camp MSS, unclassified envelope 135, IU Library, IN. Born in

Ohio in 1850, John C. Creighton enlisted in K Company on January 6, 1872, under the assumed name of Charles Chesterwood. He was discharged in 1877 at Ft. Lincoln, upon expiration of service, as a Private of good character. He reenlisted for one additional term and was mustered out in 1882 when he married Susan Andrews at Ft. Lincoln.

[2]Private Cornelius Bresnahan, K Company.

[3]Private Elihu Clear, K Company. Clear's kill site is marked incorrectly. Set in 1984 by NPS personnel, the marker was placed near the kill site of Dr. James M. DeWolf, who was slain near the edge of the bluffs. I assume that the justification for Clear's marker location was based on Godfrey's statement that Clear was DeWolf's orderly, and that he was killed near the doctor, but somewhat lower on the slope.

Unfortunately, Godfrey erred in his memory, because Clear was assigned to Lt. Hare who testified on this matter in 1879, disclosing that his orderly was killed on the east bank of the river, at the retreat crossing. It may be that Godfrey mistook Clear with Corporal John J. Calahan, also of K Company, who acted as hospital stewart to Dr. Lord and was slain with him on Custer's battlefield. I should add that the name of DeWolf's orderly was Private Harry Abbotts, of E Company, who, according to Lt. Varnum, was able to safely rejoin Reno's men on the hill upon DeWolf's death.

[4]Private William D. Meyer, M Company.

[5]Born in Montreal on September 4, 1838, Lt. Donald McIntosh was the son of Jas. McIntosh, one of the chief organizers of the Hudson Bay Company, and Charlotte Robertson, a Metis of Chippewa and English descent.

[6]Isaiah Dorman, a Negro interpreter, employed at Ft. Rice. Married to a Hunkpapa woman, Dorman was recognized and singled out by the Hunkpapas, one of whom, Eagle Robe Woman, killed him to avenge a relative slain during the valley fight.

[7]Lt. William W. Cooke, regimental adjutant.

[8]Private William J. Logue, L Company.

[9]See the interview with Charging Hawk hereafter.

[10]Sergeant John Vickory, F Company, regimental color bearer.

[11]Lt. William Van Wyck Reily, E Company.

[12]Private Charles Graham, L Company.

[13]First Sergeant DeWitt Winney, K Company.

[14]Sergeant Jeremiah Finley, C Company.

[15]Sergeant Henry Fehler, A Company.

INTERVIEW WITH JOHN E. HAMMON
[No date][1]

Hammon says Goldin[2] was one of the men who went down with Reno to find Hodgson's body. Hammon says horse Comanche lay on top where monument now stands. Keogh must have been shot off him down in hollow and the horse followed on after the rest.

Ask Hammon about ravine of water route. Was it the first break in the bluffs up river from where Reno went up? Yes. Standing on Benteen's ridge, was it the one [running] directly toward the river, or the one running diagonally down to river and in direction down river? Diagonally down river.

Hammon told of Goldin going down to river with Reno during p.m. to help bury Hodgson, when there were no Indians there. This would seem to contradict Goldin's statement about being in the timber. Hammon also said he did not think that Goldin was Custer's orderly on June 25, although [he] could not be dead sure about that.

John E. Hammon was one of the men who signed Custer's life insurance papers. He helped bury Custer.[3] Custer was shot through head in left ear, through left breast [and] through right forearm. Hammon says Benteen came in and met Reno and unsaddled.

Dead on Custer Hill: Hammon said a great many of the men were scalped and otherwise mutilated in horrible ways. Tom Custer had deep gushes in thighs and was ripped open from backbone [and] around over the bowels, so that his bowels lay open. The back of his head was smashed in. Not sure, but thinks his breast also cut open. Only way he could be identified was by the initials tattooed on his arm.[4]

Hammon said McIntosh took McCormick's[5] horse getting out of the timber. McCormick died at hospital, Ft. Meade, Sept 20, 1908, three days before I got there. Hammon said one of the heads found in the village was that of J.J. McGinnis[6] killed with Reno. Armstrong,[7] killed with Reno, was also beheaded and his head stuck on a pole.

Water party: Hammon [says] first party that went had probably the 19 men,[8] but all did not rush to water. They went down through first deep ravine through bluffs south of place where Reno crossed in retreat. The mouth of this ravine comes out at level of water in river, and 10 or 15 ft from river's edge. First party had camp kettles and these were hit with bullets. Men would work down, some carrying pails and canteens, and others guns to protect the water carriers.

About noon of the 26th second party went, about an hour later. Madden was with another water party and [was] wounded in leg. Hammon started with Windy Campbell[9] [and] took canteens and held [them] down with both hands. Had to rush to river quick and [was] then in crossfire. Campbell turned back and backed out...

Lieut. Wallace, Hare, Corporal Wallace,[10] G Troop, Private Graham,[11] G Troop, and John Hammon, G Troop, went down to meet Terry and Gibbon and their command when they came up on morning of the 27th, and Terry told them first news of Custer being killed.

Hammon met band of Rees going off with drove of Sioux ponies and mules. They passed the pack train as it was going toward Reno, after Knipe had taken message to it. Knipe also speaks of passing them.

---

[1]Camp MSS, field notes, box 3, BYU. Born in Ohio in 1855,

John E. Hammon enlisted in G Company on September 1, 1873, and was discharged at Camp Sturgis, Dakota, in 1878, upon expiration of service, as a Corporal of very good character. A copy of a signed statement, titled *The Custer Battle,* given by Hammon to Charles E. DeLand on February 28, 1898, may be found in the study collection, LBHNM, roll 11. Camp's interview with Hammon took place late in 1908. John Hammon passed away on January 22, 1909.

[2]Private Theodore W. Goldin, G Company, whose real name was John Stilwell.

[3]Hammon was assisted by Private Thomas O'Neill, whose interview follows hereafter.

[4]The extensive mutilation of Tom Custer's body was commented on by a number of witnesses. Most gruesome was the trauma to his head, which had been struck repeatedly by a blunt object, causing the skull to cave in, obliterating all facial features. The scalp had been removed down to the nape of the neck, and into the remaining cranium mass which once resembled a head, an arrow had penetrated, the point bending after impact so that it no longer could be extricated.

Since most observers described the mutilations on Custer Hill as being nil, I wonder about the reason why Tom Custer was singled out for vengeance. Could Tom Custer have been the last remaining soldier to offer armed resistance? A statement by the Cheyenne Big Beaver suggests that this may have been the case. Big Beaver pointed out to Dr. Thomas B. Marquis a location nearest the monument, on the west slope of Custer Hill, where the last man had been slain, and where Tom Custer's body was found. The following memo may also be of interest.

(George B. Grinnell note:) For many years I have been told with much mystery of the stripping of a white man on Custer field, the man having been dressed in a buckskin coat, high boots, red handkerchief about the neck and tattoo marks on wrist. This man was probably Tom Custer. I never heard who stripped him, until July 1914, when it came out it was Little Horse. The party that was stripped was found southwest of where the monument stands at the foot of a little hill... Some of the Sioux said, "This is the man who brought the soldiers," and then the Sioux women smashed his head with mauls. The man had been scalped. (George B. Grinnell Manuscript, Memo, Braun Research Library, CA.)

[5]Private Samuel McCormick, G Company.

[6]Private John J. McGinnis, G Company.

[7]Private John E. Armstrong, A Company.

[8]Reference is made to the recipients of the Medal of Honor, of which 15 medals were awarded to water carriers, and 4 medals to men who provided the cover fire for them.

(Extract from a letter by James M. Rooney to Camp, 1/16/1909, BYU:) I was not with any water party... but there was a party on the night of the 25th. It was led by a Crow Indian [Half Yellow Pace]. There was about six or seven of us [that] went with him, and I think he was the one that showed the way on the 26th.

[9]Private Charles Campbell, G Company, who was subsequently wounded while securing water.

[10]Corporal John W. Wallace, G Company.

[11]Private Thomas Graham, G Company.

INTERVIEW WITH HENRY W.B. MECHLING
[No date][1]

Graves uncovered by Grover[2] in June, 1903, some weeks before I (W.M.C.) was there. Four in one grave: Corpl. Lell of H, Meador of H, Tanner of M (alias Gephart), [and] Henry C. Voight of M, identified by Mechling.[3] Voss[4] lay nearest the river, about 200 yards from the cut bank near Crazy Horse Gully. On January 27, 1914, I saw Tom O'Neill and he told me again that the body of Voss lay across Vickory's head.[5]

Martin met us at the water hole (this may have been Knipe). Martin was leading us toward Custer when Reno came out of the bottom. We advanced to the high peaks toward Custer and found the Indians thick beyond it. Vincent Charley's remains were found by

Grover in 1903. (Mechling says Grover found a body in
the place where I (W.M.C.) know Charley was buried or
killed; so it must have been Charley's.)[6] Where Custer
lay there were horses that had been shot down and a good
many extra shells. When we first heard Reno's firing we
were perhaps 1/2 or 3/4 mile from the river and Martin
was with us. (If this be true, it clears up the question why
Martin saw no fighting or retreating in the bottom.)

On night of June 25, the Indians were crossing the
river and coming up the coulee from which they charged
later. This was one route by which they got to east of
Benteen's line. Before we four guarded the water I and
another H Co. man had gone down. Madden had been
wounded and my partner took the same camp kettle that
Madden had used, and filled it, and before he got to the
ravine it was punctured with a bullet about 3" from the
top. I filled my canteens from the kettle and could hardly
get up to Benteen's line (the hill was so steep and [I had]
several canteens strapped around my shoulders).

I asked Benteen if he wanted a drink, and he said he
would give all he was worth if he could get one. I told
him I had water, and he said: "Where did you get it?" He
drank about half a canteen full. Then the whole line were
about to start to the river for water and Benteen had to
make threats to prevent them from leaving the line and
making a break for the river.

Says Gibson[7] insisted on borrowing Mechling's carbine on evening of June 25, and Benteen advised letting
him have it. Mechling then borrowed Lell's carbine, but
it was dirty from firing and would not eject cartridges.
He then went to find Gibson and found him lying flat on
the ground, having thrown carbine away. Says Gibson
acted cowardly all through the battle.

After Benteen had a drink he said to Mechling: "Do

you suppose you could take a detail down onto that bench and guard the men who are trying to get water[?]" and I said I would try. So I took Windolph, Geiger and Voit and went down.[8] The Indians off to the north had the range on us, and when their fire got too hot we had to get to the south slope of the hill, when the Indians to the south would crack away at us and then we would run over to the north slope, and in this way kept repeating the performance. Says Benteen was the real commander on Reno Hill. Says the brush along the Little Bighorn where the men went to get water had Indians concealed, who would open fire as soon as any man ran for water.

---

[1]Camp MSS, field notes, unclassified envelope 75, IU Library, IN. Born in Pennsylvania in 1852, Henry W.B. Mechling enlisted in H Company on August 5, 1875, and was discharged at Ft. Meade, Dakota, in August 1880, upon expiration of service as a Blacksmith. He was awarded the Medal of Honor in 1878, for holding an exposed position which secured water for the command. Mechling died on April 10, 1926, and lies buried at the Soldiers Home National Cemetery in Washington, D.C.

[2]A.N. Grover was appointed Superintendent of Custer Battle-field in 1893 to fill the vacancy created by the departure of James A. Campbell, the first custodian. Grover served until 1904, when he was succeeded by W.H.H. Garritt.

[3]Corporal George Lell, Private Thomas B. Meador, Private James J. Tanner, and Private Henry C. Voight, who died during the fight for Reno Hill and who were buried in the trenches on June 27.

[4]Chief Trumpeter Henry C. Voss.

[5]See the interview with Thomas F. O'Neill hereafter.

[6]As far back as 1921, Walter M. Camp advocated the placement of a marker at Vincent Charley's kill site, at a time when General Edgerly and several other survivors could have authenticated the location. Unfortunately, it took until the early 1990s for a marker to be placed. However, the site selected is about a half of a mile farther south than the actual location, presumably chosen to better facili-tate the traffic congestion associated with an interpretive sign. Charley was reinterred in Custer National Cemetery, Grave 455.

[7]Lt. Francis M. Gibson, H Company, who was temporarily reassigned on June 28 to command G Company. For his account of the battle, titled Custer's *Last Command,* see the study collection at LBHNM, roll 3, and also his interview in Hammer, *Custer in '76,* pp. 80-81.

[8]Sergeant George H. Geiger, Saddler Otto Voit, Private Charles Windolph, and Blacksmith Henry W.B. Mechling, all of H Company, were awarded the coveted Medal of Honor in 1878, for holding an exposed position and providing cover fire for the water carriers.

Interview with James P. Boyle
February 5, 1913[1]

Says Benj. Wells'[2] body was found in the river about north or northwest of where McIntosh lay. He lay in the water on his face, with his arms spread out, and no Indians had found him, apparently, as his clothes were still on his body. Says Seafferman's [3] body was in the timber from which Reno retreated. Says John J. McGinnis had red hair and that his head was found in the village. Says Moorc[4] of Co. G was killed on the hill. Says body of Trumpeter Dose was found on flat near Ford B between two coulees (better verify this).[5]

James Boyle heard the Nathan Short[6] story and told me without prompting that he heard he was a C Co. man. Heard it was on a high hill near the Rosebud. A good many horses were killed around tepee where dead Indians were in village.

---

[1]Camp MSS, field notes, unclassified envelopes 127 and 135, IU Library, IN. Born in Ireland in 1853, James P. Boyle enlisted in G

Company on December 7, 1874, and was discharged at Ft. Meade, Dakota, in 1879, upon expiration of service, as a Private of good character.

[2]Private Benjamin J. Wells, G Company.

[3]Private Henry Seafferman, G Company.

[4]Private Andrew J. Moore, G Company.

[5]Trumpeter Henry C. Dose, G Company. On June 25, Dose served with Headquarters Staff as Custer's orderly. After verifying the evidence on Dose's kill site, Camp concluded that "Dose was slain at elevation 84 where I [Camp] thought John Briody lay." According to Camp's map published herein, "elevation 84" rises just south of Deep Ravine, a short distance from the river.

[6]Private Nathan Short, C Company, whose remains were discovered by White Man Runs Him, a Crow scout, on the divide between the Rosebud and the Yellowstone, in August of 1876. We quote here from a letter by Walter Camp to Daniel A. Knipe, 11/10/1909, LBHNM:

I have for some time been following up a line of investigation regarding Nathan Short of your company, and I am beginning to get some results. George Herendeen writes me that the body was found pinned under the horse as though the horse had fallen and the man was too weak to extricate himself. The supposition is, of course, that both the man and the horse had been wounded and that both were so weak when the horse fell that neither of them could get up. Herendeen said the Crows found the dead man and the horse near the Rosebud and down near the Yellowstone. He also states that the man had a light-colored hat with crossed sabres drawn on the front of it with pen and ink, and the number seven between the sabres. [See also the interview with Alfred W. Dale hereafter.]

INTERVIEW WITH WILLIAM G. HARDY
[No date][1]

Saw Cooke at river when Reno forded. Cooke was in

the river. Guidon that DeRudio tried to get was thrown away by Fehler[2] when he came out of the timber. Fehler had an unruly horse and could not get guidon in boot. DeRudio rode over and dismounted and tried to get it when his horse jerked away from him.

Parker and Driscoll lay on riverside of hogback on ground a little higher up than Cooke.[3] Trumpeter Fisher[4] of M Co. is the man whose stirrup Hodgson grabbed. Moody[5] killed in river on retreat. Indians charged Benteen on foot. Saw Hanley and McGuire head off the mule.[6] Saw the man on foot but did not know his name.[7]

Says only a few men between Custer and the gully. In the gully men were lying on top of one another. Could see where they ran down one side and tried to scramble up the other side. Says Comanche was not Keogh's regular horse, but one belonging to McGuiness,[8] and Keogh had him this day as an extra horse. McGuiness was left sick at Lincoln. The gray horse found on battlefield was taken to Ft. Lincoln and children used to ride him. His name was "Nap." Found Drinan's[9] horse wounded in back and he had to be killed. In 1877 Hardy was Chief Trumpeter and he was not with A Co....

French was rear guard on June 24. Old Comanche died at Ft. Riley. Dropped dead after being led to Junction City and return for exercise by Winchester. On way back Winchester rode too fast and overheated the old horse. Francis M. Reeves[10] shot through body and knocked off his horse before Hardy got mounted up. He fell off horse and got on again and rode out of bottom.

Hardy says Boss Custer was with the five cos when Reno separated, and Boss said he was going to where the fighting would be. Haddon had Boss Custer's extra pony. Boss had two Indian ponies. Hardy heard "Yankee" Korn's story. Korn[11] claimed to have rode through village, past skirmish ground, and up the bluffs. Korn told this to Hardy at the time. Heard of C Co. man found five miles from Yellowstone. Says Bustard[12] of I Co. had DeLacy's[13] horse and this horse was found dead on village side of river near ford…

Ask Hardy about shadow seen passing southward over to the east of Reno's men on hill after dark on night of June 26. Was seen by a large number of men and thought to be a body of horsemen. Some thought it was Custer or Terry and some thought it to be the Indians coming back. Trumpeter Hardy blowed trumpet calls to attract their attention.[14]

---

[1] Camp MSS, field notes, Little Bighorn, Battle of 1876, II, IU Library, IN. Born in New York in 1850, William G. Hardy enlisted in A Company on December 15, 1874, and was discharged at Ft. Meade, Dakota, in 1879, as a Trumpeter of "good character when sober." The Camp Collection at BYU contains three letters by Hardy.

[2] Sergeant Henry Fehler, A Company.

[3] Privates Edward C. Driscoll and John Parker, both of I Company.

[4] Trumpeter Charles Fisher, M Company.

[5] Private William Moody, A Company.

[6] Sergeant Richard P. Hanley and Private John McGuire, both of C Company. Hanley was awarded the Medal of Honor in 1878, for having "recaptured, single-handed, and without orders, within the enemy's lines and under a galling fire lasting some twenty minutes, a stampeded mule loaded with ammunition." Although Hanley had been assisted by McGuire, the latter was never recommended for a medal, nor was his name mentioned by Hanley when interviewed by Camp in 1910. When told of Hanley's lack of memory, McGuire responded angrily: "When he (Hanley) received his medal at Fort Meade, does he remember having made a remark like this, *'McGuire, you deserve* a medal as much as I do, if not more, for you were wounded and I was not.' This remark was made to me by Hanley before the Company." (John McGuire to Camp, 11/9/1910, Wal-

ter Mason Camp Papers, Robert Ellison Collection, Denver Public Library, hereafter cited as DPL.)

[7]Reference is made to Private Peter Thompson, C Company, who straggled behind Custer's column and who eventually turned back to join the troops on Reno Hill.

[8]Private John J. McGuiness, I Company, who had been convalescing at Ft. lincoln Hospital since May 17.

[9]Private James Drinan, A Company.

[10]Private Francis M. Reeves, A Company.

[11]Private Gustave Korn, I Company.

[12]Sergeant James Bustard, I Company.

[13]Sergeant Milton J. DeLacy, I Company, who was on detached service as Quartermaster Sergeant, at the Yellowstone Depot.

[14](Hardy to Camp, 4/3/1910, BYU:) On the morning of the 26th of June a large body of Indians were approaching us from the direction of where Custer's command was killed. The Indians wore the uniforms of Custer's men (who were all killed) and they also had some of the trumpets on which they tried to sound calls. Someone of the officers asked me if I could make out what calls they were sounding, and, of course, I could not because it was only harsh discorded blasts they were getting out of the horns. I don't remember of any trumpet calls being sounded by anyone of our trumpeters. Of course, when these Indians were approaching in our direction we thought it was Custer's command. But when they came to within about 400 yards of our lines they opened fire upon us...

On the evening of the 26th of June the Indians were pulling out for the mountains when they saw Terry and Gibbon approaching from the Yellowstone, coming to our relief. We all stood on the hillside watching them and it appeared as a long black cloud at the foot hills across the bottom, moving away. I heard Major Reno say to Capt. Moylan, ["]For God's sake, Moylan, look what we have been standing off[!"]

INTERVIEW WITH GOOD VOICED ELK
[Standing Rock Indian Reservation,] May 21, 1909[1]

Good Voiced Elk, Hunkpapa, 56 years old. Harry McLaughlin interpreter. Custer got close enough to the river to fire into and over the tepees.[2] As he was going down on the right side of the river, the Indians who had fought Reno were going down on left side, but Custer had somewhat the lead. Custer was making direct for the village as though to cross the river and come into the village, when the Indians went over and drove him back. Custer's fight started about ½ hour after Reno's retreat.

Jesse Pleets, interpreter. Good Voiced Elk says Custer's men came down to the river and were driven back upon the ridge where all were killed. Custer's men at all times were together in one body and at no time were they formed into a line or at intervals; neither did any part of them become detached for the purpose of holding any particular point. They were together in one body at all times and were killed as they were driven along. No stand was made until they got to the end of the long ridge and but few of these [soldiers] had their horses. The gray horses were all mixed in with the bays and other colors.

Those who broke from the end of the ridge and tried to get away by running toward the river were dismounted. There was a deep gully without any water in it. I saw many jump over the steep bank into this gully in their effort to escape, but these were all killed. There were probably 25 or 30 of them.

---

[1] Walter Mason Camp Papers, Ellison Collection, DPL.

[2] (Camp note:) Ben *Mato Gliunka,* Bear Lies Down, said on July 23, 1914, that Custer and his men were close enough to river to shoot into the village and were driven up onto ridge where battle took place. (Camp MSS, transcript, p. 90, IU Library, IN.)

INTERVIEW WITH MRS. HATTIE LAWRENCE
[Standing Rock Indian Reservation, 1912][1]

Mrs. Peter (Hattie) Lawrence, P.0. McLaughlin, S.D., wife of Kills Assiniboine - Hohekte, [was] ten years old in the Hunkpapa camp. An old man gave the alarm. Looking up the river he said, "Don't you see the country full of soldiers coming?" We looked up and saw a big dust. The men went and got horses in a hurry. Looking Elk[2] put me on a horse, and I rode down to Ford B and a man said, ["]Don't cross here, soldiers are coming[!"] (Says Minneconjou and Sans Arc should be transposed on my map.)[3] I looked up and saw soldiers on high ground over to the east. Saw soldiers going up a long hill in a direction away from the village, and there was no fighting until they got on top of it.

Saw many dead bodies in a deep gully, one body on top of another, the bodies looking black. No one knew we were fighting Custer. Saw a dead Indian in deep coulee among dead soldiers. Moved camp down river on the afternoon of first day and the dead were all placed in one tent. These dead were of all tribes mixed. They were all killed the first day. (She as well as some of the Minneconjou said they had been in the village only two days.) There were three, four, and five fighting men in each lodge. Camped on Reno Creek when [they] fought Crook. Dead in lone tepee was Sitting White Bear...[4]

---

[1]Camp MSS, unclassified envelope 41, IU Library, IN. Born in 1866, Hattie Lawrence was a Hunkpapa Lakota who was known among her own people as *Cankula* 'Cannonball Woman.'

[2]*Hehaca Wakita* 'Looking Elk' was a Minneconjou Lakota who was born in 1846.

[3]See Camp's map reproduced herein, which does not show the suggested correction.

[4]The Minneconjou, Feather Earring, stated that the victim's

name was Old She Bear. He added that the latter was a brother of
the Sans Arc, Circling Bear, or Turning Bear, and that he had died
from a gunshot through both hips. The Oglala, He Dog, affirmed
that the slain man was Turning Bear's brother, a Sans Arc, and that
he had died from a gunshot to the bowels. He Dog, however, did not
disclose the victim's name. This same man was known to the
Cheyennes as Plenty Bears, and to add to the confusion, Army officers were told by enlisted Oglalas in 1878, that a skull found on
Reno Creek was that of the Hunkpapa, Little Wing, a casualty of the
Rosebud Fight. Unfortunately, none of these aforementioned
names appear on the casualty list prepared by the Minneconjou,
White Bull, which may lead to the conclusion that some of these
names might have been nicknames. Additional information on this
subject was provided by the Hunkpapa, Has Horns. He told Walter
Camp in 1912 that the slain Lakota left behind on Reno Creek was
named Little Wolf, a Sans Arc, who is indeed listed on White Bull's
roster of four Lakota casualties. Has Horns added that the water-
course now known to the whites as Reno Creek was known to the
Sans Arcs as Little Wolf Creek, in remembrance of their slain
tribesman.

INTERVIEW WITH ONE BULL AND WHITE BULL
[Standing Rock Indian Reservation, 1912][1]

Say that [Sitting Bull's] twins were not born at time of
battle of the Little Bighorn, but a few days before the
battle...[2] They say when [they] fought Crook the camp
of the Hunkpapas and all others was on the Rosebud.
(They probably did not know that the Oglalas and the
Cheyennes were on Reno Creek.)

One Bull and White Bull say that a herd of Sioux
horses was driven down just ahead of Reno before fight
in bottom. One Bull saw McIntosh knocked off his

horse. Long Road - Chanku Hanska was killed 75 feet from Benteen's line. He was a Sans Arc. At point of timber in bottom Mato Washti[3] wounded before any man of Reno [was] killed. Died at Standing Rock years later. He was a Hunkpapa. We camped near mouth of Powder [during] winter before the Little Bighorn. After the battle we went up the Little Bighorn and then down the Rosebud and over to Slim Buttes. On north side of the Yellowstone [Hunkpapas] separated from the other tribes. Wintered 1876-77 between the Missouri and the Yellowstone...

Soldiers who ran from end of ridge toward river had thrown away their carbines and had only six-shooters...[4] The volleys fired by Custer may have been Custer's men firing at a charge of Indians. Dead Indians were left in village because of lack of transportation. Besides, dead Indians were often left lying in tepees as a means of burial. At times there were others than Hunkpapas in Sitting Bull's camp...

---

[1]Camp MSS, field notes, unclassified envelope 41, IU Library, IN. *Tatanka Winjila* 'One Bull,' or, 'Lone Bull' (1853-1947), and *Pte San Hunka* 'Lazy White Buffalo,' better known as White Bull (1850-1947), were the sons of the Minneconjou, Makes Room, and the Hunkpapa, Pretty Feather Woman, a sister of Sitting Bull. For biographical data on these two renowned Lakotas, see Stanley Vestal, "White Bull and One Bull—An Appreciation," (Chicago) *Westerners Brand Book* 4 (1947): 45,47-48, and also Richard G. Hardorff, *Lakota Recollections of the Custer Fight: New Sources of Indian-Military History* (Spokane: Arthur H. Clark Company, 1991), pp. 107-26, which contains White Bull's detailed account of the Custer Fight.

[2]One of these twins was accidentally left behind when the Hunkpapa noncombatants fled the village.

[3]*Mato Waste* 'Good Bear' was unhorsed in front of Reno's skirmish line by a gunshot which broke his leg. He was dragged to safety by One Bull.

[4](Camp note:) Did any witness ever talk about any of the soldiers

on ridge being drunk, and were any considerable number in that condition? He Dog says some played possum for dead, but not drunk. Bear Lying Down says some fired into the air and acted as if intoxicated. (Camp MSS, transcripts, p. 269, IU Library, IN.)

INTERVIEW WITH ONE MAN
[Standing Rock Indian Reservation, 1912][1]

Says there was a Sioux Indian in the deep gully with the 28 soldiers. At first [we] thought he was with the soldiers, but later found he was a hostile who had followed the soldiers too closely. Even our own people had mutilated the body, mistaking it for that of an Indian scout with the soldiers.[2] Says a Santee boy got Custer's horse.[3] Lone Man says there were killed seven Hunkpapas, six Sans Arcs, and three Minneconjous. He did not know how many from other tribes.[4]

----

[1]Camp MSS, field notes, unclassified envelope 41, IU Library, IN. *Isnala Wica* 'One Man,' or, 'Lone Man,' was an Oglala Lakota and a relative of Chief Red Cloud.

[2]Of the two Indian casualties sustained in Deep Ravine, one was an unidentified Oglala, while the other was Noisy Walking, a young Cheyenne.

[3](Walter Campbell note:) I [Spotted Bear] saw *Oye Maka San* (Gray Earth Track), the Santee Sioux who had the horse belonging to Long Hair. Large Pantaloons [Johnny Brughiere] told the warriors that it was Custer's mount. It was a bay with white legs and feet, and a blaze face. The horse was an excellent runner. I saw the horse in Canada when Sitting Bull and his band fled across the sacred road (*Canku Wakan*, the Canadian Line). (Judge Frank Zahn's interview with the Hunkpapa, Spotted Bear, Oct., 1923, Walter Campbell Collection, University of Oklahoma Library.)

(Zahn to Campbell, 10/15/1956:) In 1923, I made a trip to Fort Totten Indian Reservation. This was after I heard that Gray Earth Track (*Oye Maka San*) had in his possession after the Custer fight the horse Custer rode; field glasses and other items belonging to Long Hair. On the day of the battle, Custer rode "Vic." "Vic" was a sorrel, with four white feet and legs, and a blaze in the face. "Vic" was not found on the field. After the battle, Gray Earth Track went to Canada with Sitting Bull. Gray Earth Track was a Santee. When I inquired about him at the Agency, I was told that he had gone into Canada to visit. However, I was told by Good Voiced Dog that Gray Earth Track rode "Vic" into the Sioux camp, and that he had the cavalry saddle, bridle, and all the equipment Custer carried, and two white-handled pistols. This sounds quite authentic. What do you think? Gray Earth Track did not claim to have killed the man who rode the sorrel horse. This Santee also had the watch and papers which he claimed he took off the body of a soldier who wore a fringed buckskin jacket.

[4]The Indian casualties amounted to 31 adult males and 10 non-combatants. See Hardorff, *Hokahey! A Good Day to Die!*

Interview with Flying By
[Standing Rock Indian Reservation,] July 27, 1912[1]

Minneconjou chiefs were Lame Deer - Tokacha Hushte, Make Room - Kiukapi (One Bull's father), Lone Horn - He Wayzicha, Black Shield - Waha Chauka Sapa. Spotted Elk[2] was a brother of Lone Horn and at Little Bighorn was not a prominent man. We had a very large camp. There was no head chief of the Minneconjous, but four above [were] in charge of the bands, all having equal authority. Hunkpapa and Blackfeet should be in one circle. Brule and Sans Arc were camped together. Oglalas were on west side of camp and

Cheyennes on the north… Minneconjous were camped all along by Ford B, opposite Medicine Tail Coulee.

When [we] first saw Custer, the soldiers were coming down the coulee toward the village. They came down to the forks of a coulee and the command divided into two parts. One of them we chased up the hill and killed most of them on east part of the ridge. (I think by forks of coulee he means the two coulees.) More Sans Arc killed than any other tribe. Sans Arc were next in numbers to the Minneconjou. They were from Cheyenne Agency.

Last man killed was one who rode a horse and who fell near Sgt. Finley.[3] An (I think Mitch Bouyer) killed where marked (M.B.). We ran a bunch of captured horses from "D" past "K" and past "G" down to the river at "Z"[see Camp's map].[4] None of them were mounted, but as we got the horses to the river at "Z," we found a dead soldier with a six-shooter but no hat. He must have run on foot from "G." This body was within 200 feet of the river. Dog's Backbone—Shunka Chay Koha[5] killed where marked on map. Indian killed near Benteen's line was Eagle Hat, a Sans Arc—Wambli Waposta.[6]

All roving tribes staid together all summer. There should be a coulee going into the river in front of Reno's Skirmish line, as Tom O'Neill told me. After the Little Bighorn we went up the Little Bighorn to the Big Horn Mountains, thence down the Rosebud and over to Tongue and over to mouth of Powder and from there to Beaver Creek where the whole band split up. Beaver Creek flows into the Missouri River. Just after splitting up at Beaver Creek a part captured horses from soldiers.

---

[1]Camp MSS, field notes, unclassified envelope 41, IU Library, IN. Born in 1850, *Kiniyan Hiyaye* 'Flying By' was the son of the Minneconjou band chief Lame Deer who was slain by troops under

Col. Nelson A. Miles in May 1877. After the battle, Lame Deer's family returned to bury his remains, but found that the body had been decapitated, the trunk containing 17 bullet wounds.

After his father's death, Flying By surrendered at Ft. Robinson, Nebraska, and remained on the reservation until September when the unjustified killing of Crazy Horse took place. Fleeing Pine Ridge, Flying By and his two brothers joined the hostile Hunkpapas in Canada and stayed in exile for the next three years. The extreme living conditions eventually disheartened the Lakota refugees, and in 1880 Flying By surrendered at Ft. Peck and enlisted as a US Indian Scout later that year.

The Lame Deer family consisted of three sons and seven daughters. Of the three sons, Shoots Bear Running was slain during a horse-raiding party on the Crows near the Powder River in 1879. A second son, Fool Heart, died in 1882, the cause rumored to have been a broken heart from grief over the death of his father. Of the seven daughters, only two were still alive in 1912: Mrs. White Horse, on Standing Rock Reservation, and Mrs. First Eagle, on Cheyenne River Reservation.

In 1885, Chief Flying By died. This man was one of the six hereditary leaders of the Minneconjous and, being a relation of Lame Deer, the latter's son later took his name. For an earlier Camp interview with Flying By, see Hammer, *Custer in '76,* pp. 209-10.

[2]Born in 1826, Spotted Elk, better known as Big Foot, was a Minneconjou Lakota who was massacred with his band by US Troops at Wounded Knee in 1890. Spotted Elk was one of four sons born to Chief Lone Horn. Their names are: Spotted Elk, Roman Nose, Frog, and Touch the Clouds. The Lone Horn mentioned in the interview was Lone Horn's son, Touch the Clouds (1836-1905), who took his father's name upon his death in 1875.

[3]Sergeant Jeremiah Finley, C Company, whose kill site is identified on the Camp map reproduced herein.

[4](Camp note:) The statement by Flying By that he went to village with captured horses and came back and found the soldiers still fighting is more satisfactory than if he had expressed an estimate of the duration of the battle. He could not have driven the horses to the village and got back in less than 3/4 hours. This makes it reasonably certain that the fighting lasted at least an hour. (Camp MSS, transcripts, pp. 24-25, IU Library, IN.)

Point "Z" is not marked on Camp's map. However, there is a natural passage through the bluffs just north of the present park boundary, which allows easy access to the river bottom and the valley floor across. This northern ford was also described by the Cheyenne Two Moons who identified it as the location where the captured horses were taken across. I believe, therefore, that Point "Z" had reference to the aforementioned ford, near which, on the eastern slope, several artifacts have been found, among which one, .50/70 casing, a cavalry spur, and one human leg bone.

[5] *Sunka Cankohan* 'Dog's Back Bone' was a Minneconjou Lakota who was slain northeast of Reno Hill, on June 26.

[6] The name Eagle Hat appears to have been a nickname for Long Road.

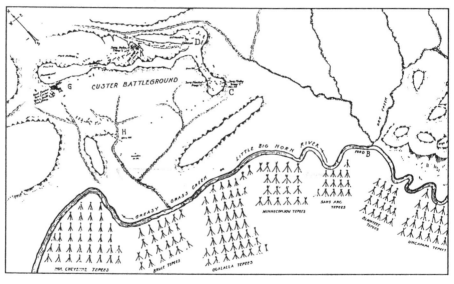

DRAWN BY WALTER M. CAMP IN 1908 AND UPDATED IN LATER YEARS
This survey map of the battlefield was based on information provided by Maj. McDougall, Sgt. Kanipe and other survivors of the fight. The dots represent markers erected at the kill sites of the slain.
Courtesy of Custer Battlefield National Monument, National Park Service.

INTERVIEW WITH CHARGING HAWK, BRULE
[No date][1]

He lives in Chicago, and who was a little boy eight years old in the camp at the Little Bighorn, says that he had often heard how, after the fight on Custer Ridge, one of the cavalry dogs was seen with a note tied to its neck, going back on the trail. The indians shot at him, but the dog escaped.[2]

---

[1]Camp MSS, field notes, box 2, Little Bighorn, Battle of 1876, II, IU Library, IN.

[2]This little dog was also mentioned by the Cheyenne Two Moons who mistakenly thought it had been killed by Indian boys. Two Moons added that the dog was yellow in color, which is corroborated by Private Burkman who referred to it as a little yellow bulldog, probably a mutt, which belonged to I Company. According to Burkman, this little dog was discovered on Custer's battlefield, sniffing each mutilated body, desperately looking for the master it had lost. This heart-wrenching scene left an indelible impression on Burkman who, being Custer's devoted orderly, had also suffered a devastating loss.

(Camp note:) [Private Francis J.] Kennedy says his name was "Joe Bush." He was a black and white bulldog. He was recovered from Indians some years after Little Bighorn. He would make friends with a soldier in uniform or an Indian, but not with a man in civilian clothes. (Camp MSS, transcripts, p. 87, IU Library, IN.)

(Camp to Gen. E.S. Godfrey, 5/19/1920:) It seems well authenticated that the bulldog of I Company, whose name was *Joe Bush*, fell into the hands of the Indians and was found among them three years later. I have been told this by several 7th Cavalry men who were there on the Little Bighorn. I think Gen. Edgerly was one of those who told me about the bulldog of I Company that the Indians captured at the Little Bighorn. Yes, Gen. Edgerly told me this. (LBHNM study collection, roll 3.)

INTERVIEW WITH THOMAS F. O'NEILL
October 13, 1912[1]

Says that Vickory lay right near Gen. Custer. Says Vickory lay on ground with face up and Voss' body lay across Vickory's head, Voss' face being down.[2] O'Neill was digging a trench to put Vickory in, Vickory having been 1st Sgt. of G Co. at one time and O'Neill had a good deal of affection for him.

While O'Neill was digging this trench, Lieut. Wallace came and said: "O'Neill, I think that will be a good grave to bury Gen. Custer in," and so Custer's body was buried in it.[3]

Tom O'Neill says that on June 28, 1876, the end of Custer ridge, where the monument stands, ran to a blunt peak. It was neither level nor sharply peaked like a hogback. South of this the ridge ran to a sharp peak, like a hogback.

---

[1]Camp MSS, field notes, Little Bighorn, Battle of 1876, IU Library, IN. Born in Ireland in 1845, Private Thomas F. O'Neill enlisted in G Company on January 17, 1867. He reenlisted on January 18, 1872, but deserted five months later. After his surrender on December 2, 1872, O'Neill served until June 19, 1877, when he was discharged at Ft. Lincoln, upon expiration of service, as a Private of good character. He reenlisted on July 15, 1877, and served until July 14, 1882, when he was discharged at Ft. Snelling, Minnesota, as a First Sergeant. After his military service, he eventually became a law enforcement officer at Washington, D.C., where he served as Sergeant of Park Police. Thomas O'Neill died on March 23, 1914. For a narrative account by O'Neill, probably given on October 12, 1908, see Hammer, *Custer in '76*, pp. 106-10, in which he stated that "he and Hammon personally dug the hole in which Genl. Custer was buried and lay the body in it."

[2]Sergeant John Vickory, F Company, who was regimental color bearer, and Chief Trumpeter Henry C. Voss. On January 27, 1914, two months before his death, Tom O'Neill reiterated to Camp that the body of Voss lay across Vickory's head.

[3](Extract of a 1908 letter by O'Neill:) I was a member of that party that buried General Custer and about from thirty to thirty-five officers and men who fell within fifty yards of him.... Some of the bodies were lying on top of other bodies; one case in particular, the body of the Chief Trumpeter, [who] was lying downward over the face of a dear friend of mine, named Jack Vickory. All the bodies were naked, except that of Vickory, which had one white sock on, with his name on it. I rolled the body of the trumpeter off Vickory and began to cover up Vickory's body. I made considerable of a mound over him, and in doing so, I made quite an excavation in the ground. Captain Wallace... said: "O'Neill, that will be a good place to bury the General." So, with the assistance of another soldier, we squared the hole, and lifted the General's body a few yards away, and placed it in the grave. (*Pacific Monthly* (July, 1908):109.)

INTERVIEW WITH JAMES M. ROONEY
[No date][1]

[Near the] gully where 28 killed, horses were lying around edge of gully. William Brown[2] and horse [found] dead in the village. Brown's body lay about 250 yards from the river and his horse further. Lay opposite Crazy Horse Gully. Says Korn's[3] story true. Says Korn came up after he (Rooney) got up with the packs. Could get nothing out of him. Asked him many questions, but all he could say was "I don't know."

Curtis, Rooney, Wm. Brown, Bruce, and Omling are the men who went back after the pack that was lost.[4] Went back about four or five miles. Rooney says Keogh was rear guard on 6/24. L Troop's packs were behind that night and gave trouble.

Timothy Reily was in F Co. in December, 1874, and was called "Pat." He is probably the one who helped

Tom Custer take Rain [prisoner]. Rooney says Isaiah lay near the timber, and some other body [lay] between that of Isaiah and McIntosh. Klein and Teeman lay in the Custer group.[5]

---

[1]Camp MSS, field notes, box 4, BYU. Born in New York City in 1848, Private James M. Rooney enlisted in F Company on December 3, 1867. He reenlisted in 1872, and was discharged at Ft. Buford, Dakota, on December 3, 1877, upon expiration of service, as a Sergeant of excellent character. The Walter Camp Collection at BYU contains four letters by Rooney.

[2]Private William Brown, F Company.

(Extract from a letter by Rooney to Camp, 2/23/1910, BYU:) William Brown was the man found in the camp. Benjamin F. Brown was killed with Reno's command. I [am] positive as to William Brown, and I [am] full sure that he was buried where he fell.

[3]Private Gustave Korn, I Company. Korn's horse bolted from Custer's column and galloped back to Reno Hill.

[4]Sergeant William A Curtiss, and Privates James M. Rooney, William Brown, Patrick Bruce, and Sebastion Omling, all F Company.

[5]Private Gustave Klein and Corporal William Teeman.

(Extract from a letter by Rooney to Camp, 4/25/1909, BYU:) There is one thing I forgot to tell you. It is about a man named Tieman [sic]. He was killed all right, but neither was he scalped, or marked in any way. His blouse was taken off and his face covered [with it].

(Extract from a letter by Rooney to Camp, 7/19/1909, BYU:) Kline [sic] was close to Tieman, and had his head crushed in with a large flat rock. [Corporal John] Briody had his right leg cut off and laid under his head. The supposition was [that he was] trying to get to Reno's command. He rode one of the fastest horses in the troop... There were two other men found in the village, but as I did not see them I will not be sure.

INTERVIEW WITH JOHN BURKMAN
[No date][1]

Was Custer's horse Vic found dead on the battlefield? Don't know. In dispute. Burkman did not go to Custer Ridge, but never heard at the time that Custer's horse was found dead on the battlefield... Did he ever hear tell of a note in Cooke's hand? Yes. Talk over with Burkman [the case of] Thompson and Watson and ask if he ever heard anything of their straggling back.[2] Never heard it before I told him...

Says Vic had three white stockings and a bald face. He was a light sorrel. Remington rifle, octagon barrel, 50 caliber, and English bulldog revolver and bowie knife was his [Custer's] equipment. He carried no sword. Vickory carried regimental colors. Dandy was dark brown with a little blaze of white in the forehead. Custer rode him since 1868. Dandy died at Monroe, Michigan, in 1890. One of his shoes is in the sisters' convent in Monroe, Michigan. About the note in Cooke's hand, Burkman heard it lay under Cooke's thigh and [that it] was handed to Lieut. Nowlan. Nowlan and Cooke roomed together and were very friendly.

Corpl. Teeman of F Troop. His body lay with [his] blouse over his face... Says Isaiah Dorman came to Ft. Pierre with Gen. Harney in 1859. He lay dead with his breast full of arrows and an iron picket pin driven through his bag [privates] into the ground, pinning him to the ground...

Says last camp on the Rosebud was on a level place of ground not near any bluff. The camp made at 2 a.m. 6/25 was at the mouth of a dry creek.

---

[1]Camp Manuscript, field notes, box 4, BYU. Born in Germany in 1839, Private John Burkman enlisted in A Company on August

30, 1870. He reenlisted in 1875, and was discharged for disability, at Ft. Lincoln, on May 17, 1879, as a Private of good character. Although Burkman was reassigned to L Company, he spent most of his service time as a personal attendant to Gen. Custer, for whom he developed an admirable loyalty. There is no doubt, therefore, that Custer's death in 1876 had a devastating impact on Burkman's life. He suicided at Billings, Montana, on November 16, 1925, and was buried at Custer Battlefield National Monument, grave site 1463 (941) A. Burkman's life was immortalized by Glendolin D. Wagner in *Old Neutriment,* a nickname given to Burkman by Custer's wife. The Camp Collection at BYU contains four letters by him.

[2](Camp to Sergt. Kipp, 11/19/1921:) I believe that he [Thompson] and Watson actually straggled back from Custer's command, for I have good evidence that neither he nor Watson were with the pack train that day (June 25). They did not fall out from Custer's command at the lone tepee, but between Reno Hill (where you made the stand two days) and where Custer was killed. On the battlefield [in 1909] Thompson did not represent to me that he got closer to where Custer was killed than about two miles. I can reconcile that part of his story very well, and I believe it. Yes, Gen. Edgerly did tell me about seeing two men join Reno's command on the hill... The men seen by Edgerly must have been Thompson and Watson. Edgerly says he shot at one of them, taking him for an Indian, but when the bullet whistled near him he waved his hat, and then Edgerly knew he was a white man. Thompson did not remember anything about the said shooting when I asked him about it. The question you raise about Thompson not reporting Custer's command killed, after Thompson joined Reno's command on the hill, is very logical. The fact that he did not do so report has always seemed queer to me. (Godfrey Papers, Library of Congress.)

———————————

Interview with Gen. Edward J. McClernand
[No date][1]

Thinks Mark Kellogg's remains found on east side of
Custer Ridge, or about where his marker now is... Says
there was a double column of fours down Medicine Tail
Coulee and turned across into dry coulee[2] and up this to
forks and then to Finley. No doubt about this being a
cavalry trail, so regular. Tepees with dead Indians toward
north end of village. About opposite Crazy Horse Gully.
Bradley discovered Custer's dead and counted 196.
[He] had been on scout in Little Bighorn valley before
fight. Was there with two companies a few weeks before
fight. Jacobs[3] and McClernand volunteered to go to
Crook, but Terry would not consent to permit an officer
to go. Says that on June 26 p.m. Terry offered Muggins
Taylor $500 to get through and communicate with
Custer. Muggins started but came back and reported
that he had met part of Custer's command and that the
soldiers had fired at him, and he was swearing and saying
that he would kill some of them the next time he would
catch them in camp. He had evidently mistaken the
Indians for Custer's men.

McClernand says where Custer monument now
stands there was a level plot 30 or 40 feet across—-not
more. This was the highest part of the ridge—in fact, it
was the top of a knoll. Going along the ridge from east to
west, there was quite a steep rise getting up to the knoll
where Custer's body lay. The bodies lay in a kind of half
circle, convex toward east. Custer's horse lay on top of
the ridge at the foot of the knoll and perhaps 100 ft from
Custer's body. It is therefore certain that the end of the
ridge has been graded down. At the time of the fight,
Custer's body must have lain as high as the top of the
monument now is.

McClernand says dead horses lay thick on the ridge where Finley lay. Says there were more than ten men between ridge and Crazy Horse Gully. Says while in camp off mouth of Rosebud heard of dead cavalry horse south of Yellowstone and not far from Rosebud. It was much talked of at the time and the conclusion was that the remains were one of Custer's command who had either straggled behind when Custer marched up the Rosebud, or had escaped from the battle of the Little Bighorn. It seems improbable that he could have been a straggler, else he would have hardly given out there, and if killed by Indians his gun would not have been with him.

McClernand has faint recollection that one of Custer's men was found in river below Ford B. Never heard that Capt. Ball[4] on his scout on Indian trail on June 28 found any dead Indians. Cannot recall any dead bodies on Cut Bank Hill or near river. At mouth of Little Bighorn on June 26 he heard the three Crows[5] call across the river, and the interpreter said they told that Custer's men had been killed like buffalo the day before.

---

[1]Camp MSS, field notes, unclassified envelope 92, IU Library, IN. A graduate of West Point, Edward J. McClernand obtained a commission of second lieutenant in the Second Cavalry on June 15, 1870, and commenced a long distinguished career which eventually earned him the rank of General. He was the recipient of a Medal of Honor for galantry in action against hostile Nez Perce Indians in the Bear Paw Mountains, in September 1877. Although he was assigned to Company G in 1876, during the Sioux War McClernand served on the staff of Col. John Gibbon as acting engineer officer. McClernand's frontier experiences are chronicled in *With the Indian and the Buffalo in Montana, 1870-1878* (Glendale: Arthur H. Clark, 1969).

[2]The "dry coulee" is presently named Deep Coulee.

[3]Lt. Joshua W. Jacobs, Seventh Infantry, who served on Gibbon's staff as the regimental quartermaster.

[4]Capt. Edward Ball, H Company, Second Cavalry.

[5]White Man Runs Him, Hairy Moccasin, and Goes Ahead. The interpreter was Bernard Prevo. Their interviews are published in Hammer, *Custer in '76*.

INTERVIEW WITH WILLIAM MORAN
[No date][1]

[Formerly of] H Co., 7th Infantry. (Scott Building, in Blind Room, Soldiers Home)... Evans and Bell [were] old and tried men, and Stewart was a recruit.[2] Engineer officer made a rough sketch of the country. Terry said [he] could not give any money (but they were actually paid a little over $100 apiece, under some other account). I heard Terry say the evening they left: "I am sorry the exigencies of the service compel us to send these men, for I fear we will never see them again." These three men were instructed to take their pick of four of the horses from the 2nd Cavalry, and they started out. F Co. of 2nd Cavalry was put across the river at Pease Bottom about 6 p.m. and escorted the men up Tullock's Fork some distance and then dropped them in the brush and let them go. This was a ruse to mislead the Indians in case they should be watching the party. They set out and same evening passed over the Custer battlefield and found dead soldiers dragged out of their graves by coyotes.

Before this Terry had tried several times to send scouts through—Muggins Taylor and Wilkinson (perhaps). We assisted carrying the wounded to the *Far West* night of June 29. Evans and Stuart came back. Bell, being very sore from riding, remained with Crook. These two met Gibbon at the Rosebud when they returned. This was by instructions of Terry, who had ordered Crook to meet him there. Started with the wounded on night of June 28 and went only across river a few miles and did not go farther than opposite Custer Ridge. Were carrying men on horse hides on poles on men's shoulders first night. On night of June 29 put the poles on mules and went rest of the way to the boat. Dropped Mike Madden onto a cactus.

Bradley had only twelve mounted men. All from 7th Infantry, two from each co. (6 cos.). These twelve men were all with him when he found Custer's body. Never heard anything about Ball's scout up the Little Bighorn reported to have found [dead] Indians in coulee. I was with the party that buried McIntosh.[3] There were a number of dead bodies not far from that of McIntosh. Says camp talk was that Reno was the first man to reach the top of the bluffs on the retreat… Says it was reported that when Benteen met Reno he asked where Custer was, and when Reno said he did not know, Benteen replied: "I wonder if this is to be another Maj. Elliott affair?"

----

[1]Camp MSS, field notes, unclassified envelope 43, IU Library, IN.

[2]Privates William Evans, James Bell, and Benjamin F. Stewart, all of E Company, Seventh Infantry, who were awarded the Medal of Honor on December 2, 1876, for carrying dispatches at the "imminent risk of life," during the period July 9 through July 25, 1876. A statement by Evans about his experience may be found in Theo F. Rodenbaugh, *Uncle Sam's Medal of Honor* (New York: Putnam's Sons, 1886), pp. 312-18.

[3]Who actually buried the remains of Lt. Donald McIntosh? In a letter dated 7/4/1876, Lt. Francis M. Gibson informed his wife that he had buried McIntosh on June 27, and that his grave was "nicely

marked." Since Gibson was a brother-in-law of McIntosh (their wives being sisters), one would naturally expect that Gibson would have arranged a decent interment for his dead relative. Major Reno, too, makes reference to the burial of McIntosh, and there is also a statement by Private Jacob Adams, of H Company, who recalled that Gibson wanted the remains brought to Reno Hill for burial in the trenches, but that the transportation of the body was made impossible due to the advanced state of decomposition, the corpse having been scorched by a grass fire. Apparently Gibson changed his mind and told Adams to bury the body where it was found. But did the remains, then, receive interment?

Members of the Montana Column tell a different story. According to Captain Henry B. Freeman and Lt. Charles F. Roe, the remains of McIntosh were buried by soldiers from the Second Cavalry and the Seventh Infantry. This statement is confirmed not only by Private Moran, but also by Sergeant Hynds, Second Cavalry, who remembered that the burial was performed by members from Lt. William H. Low's Gatling Battery and Captain William Logan's A Company, Seventh Infantry, and that the latter had made a crude headboard from a cracker box to mark the burial site. In view of this evidence, and the excerpts which follow hereafter, I am very skeptical of Gibson's statement that he had given McIntosh a decent burial, if any burial at all.

(Chas. A. Coolidge to Camp, 3/9/1911, LBHNM:) Lt. McIntosh's body, when we arrived on Reno's battlefield, laid about 20 yards from the creek, stripped naked and riddled with arrows. His horse lay beside him, bloated, and arrows sticking in the body. The right of Gibbon's line (Co. A, Logan's, to which I belonged) made camp within 10 feet of McIntosh's body and horse, which we had to move and bury at once. It was just opposite the crossing where Reno went up the hill.

(Camp to Gen. Chas. A. Coolidge, 3/11/1911, LBHNM:) Your statement regarding the remains of Lt. McIntosh is particularly interesting to me. The marker which now indicates the place where the body of McIntosh was found is about 3/4 mile from the ford where Reno crossed in retreat and about 1/4 mile from the point where Reno fought the battle in the bottom. Survivors of that fight disagree as to where Lieut. McIntosh was killed, some saying, as you do, that he fell near the river, where Reno forded and retreated up the bluffs, while others say that his body was found where the marker now is, which is about 3/4 mile from the river. Gen. Godfrey says that the marker is in the right place; that is, where the body was found.

(Chas. A. Coolidge to Camp, 3/14/1911, LBHNM:) As to McIntosh's body, I saw it and his horse to the right of where Co. A camped, and, in fact, Capt. Logan and I had to move our bivouac back a little to get away from the stench. The "star" [in the sketch below] is where McIntosh lay, and his horse lay nearer the river, with his feet to the north and, I think, his head towards the river. The body of another officer was found in the creek, or on the hill just beyond the ford, but I did not see it. There were several bodies in the creek, so I was told by soldiers who went down to get water for Capt. L. and myself. McIntosh's body was carried away from our line and buried that day we arrived; also, his horse was hauled off on account of the stench.

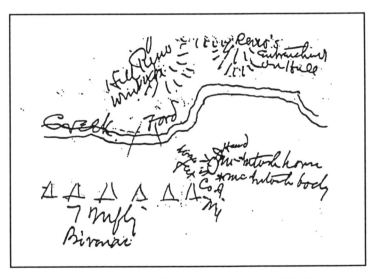

General Coolidge's Sketch of the McIntosh Kill Site.

Interview with Sergeant M.H. Wilson,
7th Infantry
[No date][1]

F Co., 2nd Cavalry, ferried over on *Josephine* and went twelve miles up Tullock's Fork with Bell, Evans and Stewart. These men had pick of 7th Cavalry horses. They went up Tullock's Fork to its source and then left the high ground southward. On second night camped on water and supposed it to be the Rosebud, but probably was not. On third night got on stream which flows south in Goose Creek and got inside of Crook's advance pickets unnoticed. Evans did talking and called for Crook, who was not present just then but arrived later, and the three men would not deliver message until they saw him personally. They had become aware of being in the vicinity of Crook's camp by seeing shod horse tracks where parties had been out hunting. They arrived in camp at 8 a.m.

Bell did not go back, being sick or sore, and did not [get] to 7th Inf again until Crook met Gibbon on Rosebud. Going back they followed some high ground until [they] struck Custer's trail. (Here they found one of Custer's dead pack mules loaded with bacon.) They followed Custer's trail and passed over Custer battlefield.

On second morning, looking through their glasses, they discovered on high ground away in distance moving objects. Could not make out whether heads of Indians over ridge or sage hens. They kept out of sight until these disappeared and then went on toward the south. They carried infantry rifle and a revolver each, 180 rounds of rifle ammunition and 60 rounds of pistol ammunition each, in belts and saddles.

Gibbon had told the men emphatically before starting

that they should keep out of sight on low ground during daytime. This they found they could not do to advantage, the ground being so rough [they] had to keep dismounting and leading horses all the time. So they kept to the top of the mountains all the way down. When they got back, they told Gibbon [they] had to cut his plan out. They kept or west slope of these mountains all the way down. These men were selected out of twelve volunteers because they were the first to volunteer. M.H. Wilson, Sgt. I Co. and Charles Hill, Sgt. H Co. had also volunteered besides the twelve.

George Herendeen called Red Stone. Roe[2] was with F Troop, 2nd Cavalry. Camped night of June 26 on bend of Little Bighorn where Crow Agency is now. On June 26 Gibbon's march was on the west side of the Little Bighorn, all the way from the Buttes east of Big Horn. Crossed Little Bighorn to its west side at these buttes about six miles above its mouth (Over this length of its course, six miles from its mouth, the direction of the stream is northwest) and then kept on west side all the way up.

At the bend (Crow Agency) next morning [they] kept over to the foothills and on the same side of the river. At the first coulee there were three or four big cottonwoods (about west of Curley's ranch) [where they] found a white man with a long beard buried in a tree. Wilson helped take him down. He was dressed as an Indian and was evidently fighting with them and killed on Reno Hill where he had been seen by soldiers. Was shot in five or six places. Mr. Willie, operator at Deer Lodge, has the bracelets [taken] off this man's hand.

Confirms Woodruff's[3] report about finding a dead man in cut in river bank with carbine and revolver and clothing all on, and the Indians had not found him (in

Reno's valley fight).[4] Says Mark Kellogg's body had not been disturbed. His clothing [was] still on, money in his pockets, and papers still with him.

---

[1]Camp MSS, field notes, Little Bighorn, Battle of 1876, II, IU Library, IN. Scrgeant Milden H. Wilson, I Company, Seventh Infantry, was a recipient of the coveted Medal of Honor, awarded to him on December 2, 1878, for deploying a skirmish line under a gallant fire by hostile Nez Perce Indians during the Battle of the Big Hole, August 9, 1877, and also for carrying dispatches at the imminent risk of life.

[2]Lt. Charles F. Roe.

[3]Lt. Charles A. Woodruff, Seventh Infantry, who commanded a gun battery of one twelve-pounder Napoleon and two Gatlings.

[4](Camp note:) Gen. Woodruff says that in Reno's retreat one wounded man took off to the left and was found dead in a little cut in river bank, not molested by Indians. (Camp MSS, transcripts, p. 78, IU Library, IN.)

(Stanislas Roy to Camp, 7/28/1910, BYU:) One particular thing that [Sergeant Samuel] Alcott told me, that I now remember was common talk in Co. for years after, was that Pat Sullivan's body was found midway in the bottom in a wash entering the river and was not mutilated and was recognized by the no. of carbine and pistol, so, naturally, the Indians did not get his clothing, and thus Sullivan must be the man referred to by Genl. Woodruff.

INTERVIEW WITH COL. CHARLES A. BOOTH
September 7, 1912[1]

Never heard where Mitch Bouyer's body was found at Little Bighorn. He [Booth] was left with Capt. Kirtland[2] and Co. B at Pease Bottom and did not get to the Little Bighorn on June 27, 1876. Says Bell, Stewart and Evans were brave men. He never heard that four Crows were sent later on the same errand. The purpose of Bradley's mounted detachment of 7th Infantry men was to reinforce the Crow scouts with white men. Does not recall that Lieut. Chas. A. Worden[3] was on the expedition at all. Never heard of the body found in the village of which Maj. Brisbin[4] wrote. Intimated that Maj. Brisbin and Capt. Grant Marsh were both unreliable as to truth and veracity.

Says Muggins Taylor did not come down the Big Horn on the *Far West* on his way with messages to Ft. Ellis. Says Taylor rode a horse, and at 4 p.m. on June 30 appeared on south bank of the Yellowstone, opposite Kirtland's camp (which was below a point opposite mouth of Big Horn) and yelled over to the camp. A small boat was then sent over after him, and he came to the camp and brought the first news of the Custer fight. He left for Ft. Ellis just after dark that same evening.

Booth says that a few days before this he saw an Indian ride out toward the Yellowstone, on the south side, chasing a buffalo toward the river. The buffalo turned and ran back toward the hills where the Indian overtook and killed it, and he cut up the meat and packed it off on his horse. He afterward investigated [the matter] and came to the conclusion that this was Curley, after he had left the Little Bighorn and before he reached the steamer (Curly verified this in his own way)...

---

[1]Camp MSS, field notes, unclassified envelope 79, IU Library, IN. Charles A. Booth was a second lieutenant in B Company, Seventh Infantry, in 1876. The Camp Collection at BYU contains a number of letters written by him.

[2]Thaddeus S. Kirtland, who commanded B Company, Seventh Infantry.

[3]Charles A. Worden, C Company, Seventh Infantry.

[4]Major James S. Brisbin, who commanded a battalion of the Second Cavalry.

Interview with Alfred W. Dale
March 2, 1912[1]

Says that he saw Curley when he came to the boat. Several [men] were trying to get an understanding of what Curley was trying to tell them, but could make nothing out. Finally Capt. Baker[2] came to me and asked if I had any of Gibbon's men among the sick, and I told him that I had a sick man, a sergeant of the 2nd Cavalry, who was pretty sick but might be able to understand the Crow. I personally took Curley to this man who understood enough Crow to make out that the soldiers Curley had been with (Custer's) were all killed. I recall the incident distinctly, as the information that Curley gave worried the sick man very much and his fever increased and he became very restless. My recollection is that Curley remained right with the boat until Gibbon's and Reno's commands came to it with the wounded.

…Says Powder River camp was on a big flat on east side of Powder and south side of Yellowstone. Dale says Custer's artillery four Gatlings; Gibbon two 12lb field pieces. Mrs. Custer went to White River on the expedition, and there the men were paid. Hobart Ryder[3] had "Kaiser" the trick horse of the 7th Cavalry, and Dale rode him a good deal. He is sure that Pandtle went[4] with Dr. Porter.[5]

Saw lots of men who saw Nathan Short's[6] remains and they wanted to know if I was going out with the ambulance to get it. A party went out and buried the remains. Sorrel horse and supposed to be one of Tom Custer's men. Found by flankers of the 20th Infantry on right flank while marching up to meet Crook in August. Was a very warm day and Gen. Otis[7] let his men put baggage on wagon train. Remains were found of both man and horse. The man's whole equipment was with him, including carbine, and was supposed to be one of Tom Custer's men...[8]

---

[1]Camp MSS, field notes, Little Bighorn, Battle of 1876, II, and unclassified envelope 131, IU Library, IN. Alfred W. Dale was a civilian employee hired as Hospital Stewart at Ft. Riley, Minnesota, and who was transferred to Ft. Lincoln to serve on the Sioux expedition of 1876. Dale was assigned to headquarters staff and served under Dr. John W. Williams, Chief Medical Officer, aboard the *Far West*. The Camp Collection at BYU contains two letters by Dale.

[2]Captain Stephen Baker, B Company, Sixth Infantry.

[3]Private Hobart Ryder, M Company, Seventh Cavalry, assigned to Dr. Williams to serve as Hospital Attendant aboard the *Far West*.

[4]Private Christopher Pandtle, E Company, Seventh Cavalry.

(A.W. Dale to Camp, 1/15/1911, BYU:) Among the names you mention I find two of men serving under my personal supervision during the Campaign. Corporal John J. Callahan—this, I am positive, is one of the men detailed as Acting Hospital Stewart under Dr. Lord. The second name is Christopher Pandtle, who was detailed as Hospital Nurse, and served under Dr. Porter (as orderly to take care of his horse, etc.), and this, I think, must be the man the Doctor refers to in his interviews.

[5]Acting Assistant Surgeon Henry R. Porter, a civilian physician.

[6]Private Nathan Short, C Company.

[7]Lt. Col. Elwell S. Otis, 22nd Infantry.

[8](Camp note:) Peter Thompson heard of Nathan Short, the C Company carpenter. He was found over on the Rosebud. The horse had been mortally wounded and had fallen and pinned the soldier to the ground, who also was supposed to have been so badly wounded as not to be able to extricate himself. He had a white hat with crossed sabres and "C"7 on front in black letters on lining of white hat. (Camp Manuscript, field notes, envelope 21, BYU.)

(Bernard Prevo to Camp, 3/23/1911, BYU:) I heard about the horse. It was on the west side of the Rosebud and the man was close by the horse. The horse was dried up when they saw it. White Man Runs Him saw the horse and the trooper. He told me about it. He said the man and the horse came from Custer's battlefield, and the horse still got the saddle on and the man was wounded.

(Camp note:) The Rees say [the body lay] near the Rosebud on high ground in some underbrush about four or five miles from the Yellowstone. When the Rees went up the Rosebud to meet Terry several pointed out the spot where the Crow scouts found the body.

(Anthony Gavin to Camp, 4/14/1914, Camp Papers, DPL:) The horse came from the Seventh Cavalry and was found on the top of a bluff, or knoll, and all below was rolling prairies, about two miles from the Yellowstone, near the Rosebud... There was nothing left of the horse [but] only part of the hide on account of the wolves and coyotes eating up same. The saddle was there, but some of the straps were cut off and taken away. Also [found was] the skeleton of an officer... [who] was a lieutenant for his shoulder straps were found with the skeleton. He fought and died on that spot... I had two of the arrows that I pulled out of the ground near the horse and gave them to a friend of mine here. No doubt they were fired into the horse. Likewise [into] the lieutenant while suffering on the ground, as there was over a dozen arrows laying around him and the horse.

(Col. Charles A. Booth to Camp, 3/9/1911, BYU:) I remember the finding of a saddled and bridled horse, about the time you speak of, but I am unable to locate the place exactly, or the time, though it was... some weeks after the Custer fight. The body of the horse laid among some sagebrush, some 200 yards from a belt of cottonwood timber; saddle, blanket, and bridle were undisturbed and in order on the body. About the feet to the left and front a carbine (Springfield) was lying; this was in perfect working order, and showed no signs of having been injured in any way and was not even rusted from exposure to weather. I have never heard of any human body being found anywhere in the vicinity, or any scout or mail carrier who was missing.

(Camp to Charles A. Booth, 3/13/1911, BYU:) It is encouraging to me to find that someone besides myself has given serious study to this incident, for the story of that horse (or horse and man) has led me on a long chase, so to speak. I have discussed this matter with a good many officers and enlisted men who were on the march up the Rosebud, including eight officers of the Seventh Cavalry who had survived the Battle of the Little Bighorn, besides Gen. Chas. A. Woodruff, Gen. Chas. F. Roe, Gen. Henry B. Freeman, Col. Edward J. McClernand, Col. R.E. Thompson, and about twenty enlisted men. All of the foregoing, including the eight officers of the 7th Cavalry, I have seen personally, except Gen. Freeman. Here are some strange things: Not one of the eight officers of the 7th Cavalry

ever heard of the matter before I mentioned it to them, yet some fifteen or more enlisted men of the 7th Cavalry were quite familiar
with the story, and most of them introduced the subject before I
asked them about it. This was rather discouraging, until I met Gen.
Woodruff and afterward Gen. Roe, both of whom introduced the
subject, before I had opportunity to do so. It seems that among the
officers of Gen. Gibbon's command this incident was quite commonly talked of at the time. Gen. Woodruff heard that only the
horse was found, but Gen. Roe recalls distinctly that the bodies of
both horse and man were reported having been found. Col. Thompson (then a lieutenant in the 6th Infantry) says that he saw the dead
horse, but no remains of a man. Gen. Freeman writes me that he
can remember nothing of the matter, whatever, neither horse or
man; that is, he had never heard of the incident until I wrote him.
Col. McClernand recalls that such a report was current, but could
not state the details. The correspondent of the *New York Times* who
was on the ground, wrote of the matter on August 7, 1876, while
Gen. Terry's command was *still lying in camp on the Yellowstone,* saying that it was expected to break camp to start up the Rosebud to
meet Gen. Crook the next day. This correspondent, also, makes no
mention of the remains of a man being found. Woodruff, Thompson, yourself and the correspondent speak only of the horse, while
all my other informants say that the remains of both man and horse
were reported... Curiously, the stories told by the enlisted men all
agree as to the report that both man and horse were found, and
some of the enlisted men I know to be truthful; others are strangers
to me... Their stories (told at diferent times and places) hung well
together, in spite of my cross questioning. If these two fellows told
me the truth then it must be a fact that a dead man and horse were
found in one place, west of the Rosebud, and a dead horse, east of
the Rosebud. There seems to be some evidence to support this conclusion. In fact, my first information, years ago, was to the effect
that there were actually two instances of finding dead bodies.
Nearly all who have told me of the man and the horse say that the
horse (dead, of course) was tied to a picket pin. Still, I am not
entirely convinced that there were two incidents of the kind, and
should further investigation result in the acceptance of only one of
these stories, and that relating to the horse without the man, there
seems to me reasonable ways of explaining either supposition,
namely, that the horse may have escaped from the Custer fight

alone and wandered that far; or he may have been ridden that far by a wounded soldier who had escaped from the fight with him.

(Charles A. Booth to Camp, 3/15/1911, BYU:) If I said before that the find [of the horse] was east of the Rosebud, that was *correct;* if I said *west*, it was an error of orientation... I stood beside the carcass of the horse with a group of 7th Infantry officers; our stay there was long. We were marching parallel to a line of cottonwood trees or dense underbrush, across a sagebrush plain. We halted for a brief time, and I went to my left to join the rest of the officers about the horse. The body of the horse lay nearly parallel to the timber, and the carbine to the left of and in front of the horse. The saddle and blanket were in proper place on the horse's back. I believe Captain [Walter] Clifford stood on the spot where the carbine was lying. The carbine was in good working order. No human body was in sight, and I never heard or could learn of one being found. I remember Capt. Clifford, 7th Infantry, in our group and (I think) Capt. [William R.] Logan and Lieutenants [Alfred B.] Johnson and [George] Young, but of these, only Young (now Colonel) is alive. So far as I know, only the command of Gen. Gibbon, 7th Infantry, ever *saw* the body.

(Camp to Charles A. Booth, 3/20/1911, BYU:) The stories I have heard about the man and the horse have it that both were badly decomposed and that the horse was about half eaten by coyotes, which would indicate that they had been dead some weeks. I am now inclined to think as you do, that the dead horse that you saw did not wander there from the Custer battlefield alone, admitting that that was the starting point. Since reading your letters I am about ready to form another conclusion, and that is that the stories of the dead horse, in the one case, and the dead man and horse, in the other case, did not originate with the same "find." Before reading your letters I had expected to run all of these stories down to a common origin. Altogether, I have had lengthy and careful interviews concerning the battle of the Little Bighorn with about 17 or 18 Sioux and Cheyennes who were in the fight. One of these told me that some time after the battle a small party of Sioux, detached from the main body, ran across a man on the Rosebud and killed him. He was dressed in soldier's clothes that were badly worn and had been catching frogs, having several dead ones in his pockets. He stated explicitly that the man was not mounted, and they were at a loss to understand how he came to be where they found him. I have never thought much about this story, although everything else that the

Indian told me seemed to be straight. In order to connect this man with the dead horse that you saw it would have to be presumed that the horse had gotten away from him and had gone some distance, for if the horse had been near the man killed, the Indians would have taken the carbine and saddle.

(Camp to Charles A. Booth, 3/29/1911, BYU:) It now occurs to me more clearly than before that if there were two finds at about the same time—a man and a horse in one place, and a horse in another —it would have been an easy matter for the accounts of the two incidents to have become more or less mixed or confused in subsequent recitals.

(Editorial note:) Additional material on this matter is included in a forthcoming sequel to *Custer Battle Casualties* to be published by Upton and Sons.

Interview with Gen. Fred D. Grant
March 22, and April 19, 1910[1]

Gen. Grant, in summer of 1878,[2] soon after the bodies scattered about the field had been disinterred and permanently buried at the north end of Custer Ridge, where the monument now is, found several empty graves on Greasy Grass Hill. As well as he could remember there were four or five of them scattered about over some distance on this hill, part of them, at least, being rather on the south slope of the hill, but well up toward the top. These empty graves had the same general appearance as those scattered all over Custer Ridge and now located by markers, there being rank grass, fragments of clothing and other indications that bodies had been temporarily buried where the dirt had been thrown up.[3] This is the very evidence by which the markers were placed in 1890.

The evidence of fighting at various points was so clear at that time that he formed the following theory or conclusion as to how the fight had progressed: Custer had come down Medicine Tail Coulee and turned to the right, out upon the flat next to the river, as though to cross into the village. Presumably the first firing from the village side was from the fringe of timber or brush along that side of the stream, while the troops occupied this flat. This fire may have been so strong as to cause the men to hesitate, and, at all events, they had moved to Greasy Grass Hill, as a more commanding position, only to find it dominated by higher ground to the north, with Indians advancing up the river from that direction also, which would account for the presence of dead bodies here.

Leaving this hill and passing a slight depression, they reached higher ground where the group of bodies, including those of Sergeants Finley and Finckle,[4] was afterwards found. Here again they saw unoccupied higher ground still to the north, beyond a slight depression, and they had gone to it, the evidence of dead bodies marking the trail to where the Calhoun and Crittenden[5] markers now are. It then impressed him that the men whose bodies lay along the route had probably been killed by fire from the rear or left flank.

On Yellowstone expedition when [they] got to Glendive Creek he went down Yellowstone to Ft. Buford in a skiff to carry dispatches to order up more supplies. The Indians had been sighted all around and he considered it an adventure. For this reason he did not get further on the expedition.

In 1878 he went from Ft. Custer to Custer Battlefield. Saw where McIntosh had been buried and remains removed, and [saw] other graves around it and not far away. On hill at cut bank just below Ford B he saw several graves from which bodies had been only recently removed. They were on the east slope of [the] hill, but [he] cannot recall distinctly whether near top of hill or not, but thinks they were near top. He is certain they were there and [is] not confused with graves on Battle Ridge.

---

[1]Camp MSS, field notes, Little Bighorn, Battle of 1876, and Battle of 1876, II, IU Library, IN. Frederick Dent Grant was born in St. Louis on May 30, 1850, and was the son of President Ulysses S. Grant. A graduate of West Point, Frederick Grant received a commission as Second Lieutenant in the Fourth Cavalry on June 12, 1871, and commenced a military career which eventually earned him the rank of Brigadier General, USA in 1901. The Camp Collection at BYU contains a letter by Grant.

[2]From March 17, 1873 till June 1, 1881, Grant served as an Aid-de-Camp to Lt. General Philip H. Sheridan who, with his staff, visited Custer's battlefield on July 21, 1877. However, Grant's interview refers to a visit in 1878, which date may not be correct either since the remains spoken of by Grant were not exhumed until July of 1881 when Lt. Charles F. Roe reinterred the bones in trenches around the base of the monument.

[3](Camp to Gen. Charles A. Woodruff, 4/22/1910, LBHNM:) Just north of Ford B, on the east side of the river, is a flat, and just north of this flat is a cut bank and a high bluff. This is the bluff where you and I think Custer should have made his stand and fought his battle. For convenience of reference, let us call this bluff, at its south end, where it comes out to the river over the cut bank, Greasy Grass Hill. Across the flat to Greasy Grass Hill, is 1800 or 1900 feet, more or less, depending upon what point one selects as the foot of the hill. Curley *does* say that Custer remained a short time on the flat, near the river and just south of Greasy Grass Hill, before starting for Custer Ridge. I could not, however, get from him much of an idea as to the length of time Custer and his command stopped here. (You know how difficult it is to get an Indian to estimate time according to our standards.) He is rather hazy as to what was done while Custer was on this flat, except that he says that shots were exchanged by both sides across the river at this point, the soldiers firing into the village and the Sioux firing at the soldiers in return.

From all that Curley told me about the shooting at this point, I do not think that he (Curley) got as near the river as did the soldiers. I just surmise this from the fact that he is so indefinite about matters. About what happened on the retreat up to Custer Ridge and the fighting on the ridge, he is more explicit. I want to tell you that I think considerable fighting was done by soldiers right on top of Greasy Grass Hill, but whether all of Custer's men were up there or not, I am not clear. I rather think that only part of them were there. I am accepting the statement of Mr. [Fred] Server that dead bodies were found up there, and there is reliable evidence to support him, but not as complete as I would like to have it. I intent to be more specific about this point the next time I interview the Sioux. It did not seem as important to me two years ago as it does now.

(Camp to Peter Thompson, 4/24/1910, BYU:) You will probably remember where we ate dinner in the wagon last summer, after tramping along these bluffs, Knipe having driven on ahead of us and stopped on the flat between the mouth of that coulee [Deep Coulee] and the hill, or bluff, over the cut bank. The bluff near which we ate dinner is the one where you and [Private James] Watson saw the five companies just before the battle started. Gen. Grant says that when he visited there in 1878, there were four or five graves right on top of that bluff, just where you have told me that Custer's fight started. An enlisted man who was in the 2nd Cavalry and who came in with [Col. John] Gibbon, also tells me that he saw five dead bodies up on that bluff on June 28, 1876. This man of the 2nd Cavalry is Mr. Server, who keeps hotel at Crow Agency, as you may remember. You and Server and Gen. Grant, therefore, seem to agree pretty well as to where Custer's fight started.

(Editorial note:) A site excavation on Greasy Grass Hill in 1985, yielded a lower torso, including a pelvis and bones of both legs, with a cavalry boot still attached to the right leg. Nearly one hundred casings from both friendly and hostile fire have been discovered in the same general area over the past years.

[4]Sergeants August Finckle and Jeremiah Finley, both of C Company.

[5]Lt. John J. Crittenden, 20th Infantry, on detached service with L Company, Seventh Cavalry.

Appendix

Odometer used on hub of wheel, July 31, 1911. Diameter of wheel 42["]. Cir. 11'1¼" 475 RPM.

	[Running Revolutions]	[Dist. Between Points]	[Running Mileage]
Corral	4730	0	0
2 a.m. camp	4030	1.47	1.47
Divide	2487	3.25	4.72
Spring	1090	2.94	7.66
End of ledge of rock	8992	4.42	12.08
Coulee from S.E.E. of Benteen water hole (This probably the one Benteen came down with 3 cos.)	8992	0	12.08
Benteen watered horses	8465	1.11	13.19
Lone Tepee	7910	1.17	14.36
Ford A	6377	3.23	17.59
South end of Benteen line	5700	1.42	19.01
Benteen intrenchment	5656	.09	19.10
K Company line	5600	.12	19.22
Retreat Point	5460	.30	19.52
Sharpshooter Hill	5437	.04	19.56
Vincent Charley Coulee	5190	.52	20.08
Mouth of South Coulee [Cedar Coulee]	4890	.64	20.72
Where Martin probably left Custer	4452 or 4600	.61 or .92	21.33 or 21.64
Where Custer turned to right out of Medicine Tail Coulee	4060	.82	22.46
Custer nearest river	3955	.22	22.68
Sgt. Butler	3940	.04	22.72
Finley marker	3660	.58	23.30
[Totals]	11070	23.30	23.30

The odometer readings are contained in the Camp MSS, field notes, unclassified envelope 92, IU Library, IN. The corresponding mileage figures were computed by the author. It should also be noted that Camp's starting point was at the Finley marker, on Calhoun Ridge, and that he ended his measurements east of the divide. I have reversed Camp's listing in order to show the flow of motion of Custer's regiment on June 25.

Index